The Animal-Friendly Cookbook

On the Way to Nature

The Animal-Friendly Cookbook

On the Way to Nature

Commissioned for publication by the

Gabriele-Stiftung

Gabriele-Foundation
The Saamlinic Work of Neighborly Love
for Nature and Animals
Your Kingdom Come – Your Will Is Done
Pray and Work

The Sanctuary Land
A Home for Animals

First English Edition 2008
Published by:
© Universal Life
The Inner Religion
P.O. Box 3549
Woodbridge, CT 06525
U S A
www.Universal-Spirit.org

Licensed edition
Translated from the original German title:
„Das tierfreundliche Kochbuch – Hin zur Natur"

From the Universal Life series with the consent of
© Verlag DAS WORT GmbH
im Universellen Leben
Max-Braun-Strasse 2
97828 Marktheidenfeld / Altfeld
Germany
Order No. S 436en

The German edition is the work of reference for all
questions regarding the meaning of the contents

Photos pp. 5, 19, 21, 23, 25, 27, 29, 31, 33, 35, 39, 41, 45, 47, 49, 51, 53, 63, 67, 73, 75, 77,
85, 89, 93, 99, 101, 105, 107, 109, 111, 113, 121, 123, 135, 137, 147, 149, 151, 153, 159, 165,
169, 177, 179, 181, 187, 189, 191, 197, 204, 205: Christian Teubner

Fotos S. 57, 59, 61, 163, 171: Christine Fleurent

Photos pp. 13, 15, 17, 37, 43, 55, 65, 69, 71, 79, 81, 83, 87, 91, 95, 97, 103, 115, 117, 119,
125, 127, 129, 131, 133, 139, 141, 143, 145, 155, 157, 161, 167, 173, 175, 183, 185, 193, 195 199,
201, 203, small pictures and illustrations: Verlag DAS WORT GmbH

Printed by: McDonald & Eudy, Inc.
Temple Hills, Maryland 20748

ISBN: 978-1-890841-57-7

Table of Contents

The Animal-Friendly Cookbook

wants to contribute to the fact that ever less animals,
which are our fellow creatures, have to suffer under
human beings.
We want to ease the adjustment particularly for those people
who would like to refrain from eating meat, by offering them
a large variety of tasty recipes.

All recipes and instructions should be considered only suggestions
and recommendations that can be altered to suit the cook's fancy.

The profits from the sales of the
Animal-Friendly Cookbook
are applied by the *Gabriele-Foundation*
The Saamlinic Work of Neighborly Love for Nature and Animals.

There is some brief information on the *Gabriele-Foundation*
in the foreword and on page 207.

Introduction

Haven't you often thought: "We should really go without eating meat. I really should give it a try…"? We often hear: "Without meat – that's not really a meal!" And yet there is an interesting and convincing alternative. The recipes in this cookbook for animal lovers prove this. Something that is healthy and tastes good doesn't have to be complicated and lavish. There are countless variations and possibilities. There's room for your creativity and individual preferences – and in this way, cooking can become a pleasure!

And it's not only good for you and your loved ones, but also good for the animals.

Not from one day to the next …

It's not surprising, when some people find it difficult to change their way of thinking. When the good intentions of someone – who has a reasonable point of view that says: "I really shouldn't eat meat anymore" or "not so much meat" – don't lead to results, then it's usually because years of well-nurtured and cultivated programs stand in opposition to this. And the word "really" in the above statement indicates how stubbornly ingrained eating habits assert themselves.

In our society, prepared meat is usually still the core of a good wholesome meal. The dish is also usually named after the meat used. People who live a vegetarian way of life are leniently smiled upon, or one considers them fanatical improvers of the world. "And, after all, Jesus also ate the Easter lamb, that is, meat."

But what really happened at that time, Christ tells us today in His great work of revelation, *This is My Word. Alpha and*

Omega. The Gospel of Jesus. The Christ-revelation that has meanwhile become known to true Christians all over the world:

Neither the apostles nor the disciples gave the order to slaughter a lamb. But as a gift of love, parts of a prepared lamb were offered to Me as well as to the apostles and disciples. With this, our neighbors wanted to make a gift for us, for they did not know better. … I instructed My own that man should not willfully kill an animal nor should he consume the meat of animals which were killed for the consumption of their meat. However, when people who are still unknowing have prepared meat as nourishment and make of it a gift to the guest, offering it with the meal, then the guest should not reject the gift. For there is a difference whether a person consumes meat because he craves for meat or as a token of gratitude to the host for his effort. (pp. 786-787)

So, where does the disdain for animals come from?

Many people love animals, and yet many animal lovers also eat meat, because it's simply what we normally do in the Christian western world. Actually, this barbarism against animals can ultimately be traced back to reports in the Old Testament, in which God allegedly advised priests to cruelly slaughter and sacrifice animals. The priests were then allowed to consume a part of the meat. The priests of today also eat a lot of meat – particularly on church holidays. However, today they do not slaughter the animal themselves, but have others slaughter it and the church Christians who follow them do the same.

This is not very Christian, however, because Jesus, the Christ, loved not only human beings, but every animal, every plant, every life form. In *This Is My Word*, He tells us today through Gabriele, the prophetess and spiritual ambassador of God for our time, among other things, the following:

The whole of infinity is serving love, serving life. Man, too, is called by Me, Christ, to serve his neighbor in a selfless way. This also includes his second neighbor … The animal cannot speak. It suffers and endures silently and can hardly express it's pain and grief. (pp. 201-202)

Therefore be considerate, kind, sympathetic and friendly not only with your own kind, but also to every creature which is within your care; for you are as gods to them to whom they look up to in their need. (p.180)

What Jesus taught and Himself lived as an example, Christ is teaching again today. In many revelations and in countless hours of spiritual schooling, He makes clear to us via Gabriele what it is that will lead us out of our burdened and egotistical existence and into a fulfilled and peaceful life, in which higher ethical and moral values come to bear fruit more and more. The more a person examines his character traits and reduces his passions, of which eating meat is also a part, that is, the more a person ennobles himself by the "do-no-more," the more his sensory perceptions will become finer, and his bad habits, which include eating meat, will fall away from him, as it were. He changes himself to the better, and his life on Earth will be a gain in every aspect, also in regard to the animals.

A fine sensory perception results in an alert character, an awareness, that not only reflects a person's positive aspects, but in which the animals and all forms and forces of nature are at home.

Out of this grows the need for living food, for vegetable food like bread, fruit and all kinds of vegetables. The consumption of animal carcasses gradually stops. The transition from a meat diet, that is, from dead food, does not, of course, happen from one day to the next.

This animal-friendly cookbook is an unusual cookbook, because the recipes you find in it were made using produce from peaceable cultivation. What does peaceable cultivation mean? The farmers of the New Jerusalem farms use neither solid nor liquid manure on their fields. They use no poisons, no artificial fertilizer of any kind, and they also give the fields natural mineral substances, which every person needs in order to remain healthy and emotionally stable. These include natural nitrogen, potassium, phosphorus, calcium, magnesium, iron, manganese, selenium and many other trace elements.

Anyone who has a heart for nature and animals is already well on his way to health and top performance with this cookbook.

Beyond this, by purchasing this book you are helping the animals and nature very concretely and directly. How?

This animal-friendly cookbook is published under the auspices of the *Gabriele Foundation, the Saamlinic Work of Neighborly Love for Nature and Animals.*

The goal of the *Gabriele Foundation* is to allow the soil, the fields, meadows and forests to develop as originally intended by the Creator, God, and to create a healthy fellowship among human beings, nature and animals. In this way, the Earth will become healthy and give good, healthy, happy fruit in abundance. And from this, human beings and animals receive the life force that keeps them healthy.

Original Christian farmers have worked the fields for years now in a peaceable way. It is much more than "organic"; it is a peaceable, natural agriculture. They deliberately refrain from using all those things people have thought up for "living well" at the cost of nature and animals.

One of the farmers working on the farm, which is located on the edge of the South Spessart region of Germany, explains to us how it is done:

"We respect and care for nature. On our fields nature is allowed to remain nature. The plants are respected as living beings and are allowed to grow in a natural way. The fields and produce belong to the "family" and this is why the farmer treats them with care.

We are friends of nature. Companion plants (generally known as weeds), insects and other animals are useful creatures. They work as nature's helpers and support a healthy soil life.

Our fields are chosen carefully, cultivated and cared for. Many aspects are carefully considered: the stones on the fields, the channeling of water, the water-retention capability, the orientation of the field to the sun, previous crops, organism activity in the soil and much more. The working of the field in autumn and in spring is done in consideration of the plant that is targeted for that field. And the selection, care and preparation of the seeds and seedlings are important factors so that the plants may flourish.

There is a constant push to fertilize in agriculture – but not with us! When the fields are treated naturally, there is no exploitation – there is a giving and receiving in mutual respect. We see the earth as a living organism that has the right to an honest and open communication. Every coercive measure – killing the soil's living organisms, violently breaking up the soil's crust, applying fungicides and pesticides, as well as measures whose goal is gaining the highest yield possible from the soil – have no place here. We put no substances in the soil that kill life, and which the person then has to ingest with his food. And we do not practice genetic manipulation!

Two years planting, one year fallow – three year crop rotation. We give the field only the natural and nutritive sub-

stances that it lacks, because it is a living organism.

Communication is also very important. A friendship between human beings could hardly be built up and maintained without small acts of kindness, without being aware of how you could do something good for your friend or something that would make him happy. The same applies to the fields that give us food, and thus life's sustenance.

All this goodness would not be possible if the farmer himself did not have a peaceable attitude, for all life reacts to the radiation of those involved. Our farmers have striven for years to live and work according to the Ten Commandments and the advice of the Sermon on the Mount of Jesus and so they can offer their customers real products from peaceable agriculture."

The agricultural products then make their way to other enterprises of the Original Christians where they are processed. They are then sold at numerous markets in larger and smaller cities of Germany as well as a Mail-Order House – *Lebe Gesund Versand* – that pass on the ex-

cellent products to customers who appreciate genuine, good, pure nature. Let's follow the path from kernel to bread:

We harvest the grain immediately upon ripening, and dry it with care. It is then stored in its best condition without the application of any chemicals. And we see to it that not a kernel of grain is lost. For we owe this to nature.

We do not beat the grain, but grind it gently on our stone mill and this means we grind the whole grain with the germ, even with white flour. We do not produce sourdough; our sourdough comes from nature. Our bread is not made up of "ecological components" – it is nature! Through a natural ripening process, the nutrients that are so important for the energy of our human constitution become available in an optimal way. This produces an easily digested, wonderfully aromatic bread, which keeps a long time when stored correctly.

This is how clear, friendly, tasty food for a healthy life is produced. Every slice of bread is a friendly gesture of nature. Every bun is the smile of a large grain field, every spice, the breath of nature.

The Work of Neighborly Love for Animals and Nature – A Step into the Kingdom of Peace of Jesus Christ

All this – the what and the how – and much more, was not dreamed up by people. It went out from the one eternal Spirit, God, who *has again sent a great prophet to us people, the prophetess and spiritual ambassador of God, Gabriele.*

Gabriele not only gave and gives to her fellow man the truth of the heavens, the word of God, in revelations and spiritual teaching hours, but she has worked for a life of people who are in consonance with nature. (From the brochure *The Gabriele – Foundation*, pp. 2-3)

In the great work of revelation *This Is My Word*, Christ tells us:

Feel the unity with each creature and with all stones and plants and protect the life that is entrusted to you! ... Behold, nature, the life of creation, provides for you. (pp. 180-81)

From this awareness, developed peaceable agriculture, which means:

Whatever nature gives to us we should consider as a gift of nature for human beings and the animals. "The conventional attitude is that nature stands under human jurisdiction," one of the farmers explains. "People take from this the right to breed animals, to eat them and to exploit them for their own purposes without limitation. On the other hand, if a person sees himself as a part of nature, then he would

10

never think of breeding animals or torturing them, because he knows that he would be doing all this to himself."

The purpose of the *Saamlinic Work of Neighborly Love* is also *to create a living space for the animals where they can lead a life that is worthy of free creatures of God, where they can move freely and at peace according to the needs of their species – without fear of being chased and hunted down; in a growing positive link with people who bring them help and care in respect, appreciation and friendship in their feelings, thoughts and selfless deeds.* (p. 4)

Whoever is interested to know more is invited to read the brochure *The Gabriele Foundation. The Saamlinic Work of Neighborly Love for Nature and Animals*, which can be ordered free of charge from *The Gabriele Foundation.*

Expressed briefly: Introduced by God, the Creator of the universe, a Kingdom of Peace for the Earth, nature and the animals is developing on a small part of the Earth. It is presently small, comparable to the seed of an oak, but it will grow, for many people all over the world are being addressed by what is taking place here. They recognize the greatness that is in the making and they feel in their hearts that the Kingdom of God, which has been prayed for in the Lord's Prayer for two thousand years, will come in the words "*Your kingdom come, Your will be done,*" not in a far away utopian future, but is already being built now. And many who recognize this contribute to it, because more woods, meadows and fields should be acquired in order to expand the peaceable habitat for animals and nature. And the proceeds of this animal-friendly cookbook will also be used to buy a few acres of land for the animals and for nature – which is at the same time a small building block for the Kingdom of Peace.

And so, what you are holding in your hands is not simply a vegetarian cookbook. It is much more – it is a part-aspect of an event of cosmic proportion, which is occurring at this time on the Earth. Now the decisive milestone is being set in the turn of time from the old, materialistic time into the era of Christ. This became possible because Gabriele, the great messenger of light of the heavens, is among us.

The Kingdom of Peace and of love, which the prophet Isaiah announced, of which Jesus of Nazareth spoke, and which has almost been forgotten for 2000 years, is now being built.

The path with which we can achieve peace with ourselves, with our fellow man and with the Earth, with nature and the animals, is the Inner Path. It does not lead us to a person but it is the path with Christ to God.

Christ says in the *Great Cosmic Teachings of Jesus of Nazareth:*

He, the great All-One, transferred to Me the task to guide back into the eternal Being all that seemed lost.

In Me and with Me, you shall mature into the eternal life, where I Am in the Father, just as you, too, are with Me in the Father ...

I Am the life, Christ, the Son of God. The one who lets Me, the Spirit of Life, Christ, rise in him has found his spiritual heritage again, which is his eternal life. Then the being returns home to God, the eternal Father, because it is from Him.

All will resurrect in Me. I will find all those who believe they are lost. And the weak will grow strong in Me, for I Am the glory in the Father. (p. 17, *Great Cosmic Teachings...,* pocketbook edition)

*T*his introduction is quite unusual for a cookbook. And yet, through it, you, too, may come to know about what is taking place today, in our time: In His word, God, our eternal heavenly Father extends His hand to us. In His word lies His all-permeating power, the primordial power, His wisdom and goodness and His guidance for every single one.

Apples

»We give you our life energy!«

    I am an apple with a golden heart – brimming with the energy of life! I give you the strength of the good earth, the freshness of the water, the dynamism of the wind, the radiant power of the sun: pure nature, without solid or liquid manure, without sewage sludge, without chemicals, just as I grew and ripened on the Farms of New Jerusalem!

    With me you can prepare not only sweet dishes, but also delicious spicy ones. If eaten raw, my crispness and aromatic flavor will please you, and I will give you many vitamins and minerals.

"Heaven and Earth"

4 Servings

4-5 medium potatoes

1 c. water (250 ml)

4-5 medium apples

1 tbsp. sugar

2 medium onions

4 tbsp. sunflower oil

Salt to taste

Preparation time:

Approx. 50 min.

Serving suggestion:
Serve with a green salad and cider, apple juice, or a white wine mixed with sparkling water.

1 Peel and dice the potatoes. Quarter and core the apples.

2 Simmer potatoes in water, 10 min. covered. Add apples, sprinkle with sugar and simmer 20 min. on low heat.

3 Heat sunflower oil in frying pan, add chopped onions and sauté until golden yellow.

4 Mash potatoes and apples together with a potato masher and flavor with salt. Place mashed potatoes and apples in a serving bowl, cover with sautéed onions and serve at once.

Stuffed Apples

4 Servings

4 large apples

4 large onions

4 tbsp. sunflower oil

5 tbsp. sesame seeds

Salt to taste

Pepper to taste, freshly ground

1 tbsp. fresh marjoram

Preparation time:

Approx. 60 min.

Preheat oven 350° F (180° C)

Serving suggestion:
Serve with
small boiled potatoes and
a fresh green salad.

1 Peel apples, cut in half and core. Peel and thinly slice onions.

2 In a frying pan sauté onions in oil. Add sesame seeds, marjoram, salt and pepper.

3 Cover bottom of an ovenproof dish with 4 tbsp. onion-sesame seed mixture. Place apple halves on top.

4 Fill apple halves with remaining onion-sesame seed mixture and bake in oven 30 min.

Apple-Potato Pan

4 Servings

2-3 small potatoes

2-3 small apples

1 small onion

8 tbsp. sunflower oil

¼ tsp. salt, or to taste

1 tbsp. fresh marjoram

Preparation time:

Approx. 30 min.

1 Peel potatoes and apples and cut into large slices. Peel onion and slice into thin rings.

2 Heat oil in frying pan. Sauté onion in hot oil until translucent, add potatoes, then apples, and cook until potatoes are tender. Season with salt and marjoram.

Indian Curry

4 - 6 Servings

1²/₃ c. long grain rice (300 g)

2½ c. water (600 ml)

4 large onions

2 medium apples

1-2 bananas

2 tbsp. raisins

2 heaping tbsp. flour

1²/₃ c. rice or oat milk (400 ml)

4 tbsp. sunflower oil

2-3 tbsp. curry powder

1 tsp. chili powder, or to taste

Pepper, freshly ground

Salt to taste

3 tbsp. slivered almonds

Preparation time:

Approx. 35 min.

Variation:
Add pineapple chunks and coconut milk. Serve with flavored black tea.

1 Add rice to boiling, salted water. Stir, bring to a boil. Remove from heat, cover and let stand 25 min.

2 Finely chop onions. Core apples and cut into small pieces. Peel and slice bananas. Rinse raisins.

3 Lightly toast almonds in a dry frying pan until golden brown. Set aside on a plate to cool.

4 Heat oil in frying pan. Sauté onions in hot oil, stirring rapidly. Add curry powder and cook 5 min.

5 Add flour and mix well. Add rice or oat milk, bring to a boil. Add apples, bananas and raisins and mix well. Cook on low heat 5 min. Add water if necessary.

6 Season to taste with salt, pepper and chili powder. Garnish with toasted almonds. Serve in preheated bowl with rice.

Apple Rings

4 - 6 Servings

4 medium apples

3 tbsp. sugar

1 tsp. cinnamon

Frying oil

For the batter:

½ c. beer or sparkling water (100 ml)

2 tbsp. sugar

1 tsp. cinnamon

½ c. oat or rice milk (100 ml)

4 - 5 heaping tbsp. flour

1/8 tsp. baking powder

Pinch of salt

3½ tbsp. vegetable shortening, melted but not hot

Preparation time:

Approx. 50 min.

1 Peel, core and slice apples into ⅓ in. (1 cm) rings. Mix 3 tbsp. sugar and 1 tsp. cinnamon.

2 Sprinkle rings with sugar-cinnamon mixture and set aside for 30 min.

3 Batter: Mix all ingredients using wire whisk or mixer until smooth. Dip sugar-cinnamon coated apple rings into batter.

4 Heat shortening in frying pan. When hot, fry apple rings until golden brown. While still hot, coat rings again in sugar-cinnamon mixture. Enjoy warm or cold.

Coconut-Vanilla Sauce

4 - 6 Servings

1 c. coconut milk (250 ml)

1 tbsp. cornstarch (or wheat starch)

2 tsp. sugar

Water

¼ c. margarine (60 g)

1 tsp. vanilla

Preparation time:

Approx. 20 min.

1 Put coconut milk, vanilla and sugar in a pan, mix and bring to a boil. Mix starch with a small amount cold water and add to coconut-milk mixture.

2 Cook for a few min., stirring constantly. Remove from heat, add margarine, and mix well until melted. Flavor with vanilla.

Artichockes

»I have a good heart – for you«

I delight you with a delicate flavor, and raw or cooked, I give a lot of good things to your body: folic acid, vitamins, copper, iron and more. And my bitter essence is invaluable for you.

Since I grew from the peaceable cultivation of the farms of New Jerusalem you know my worth – and you will taste it, too! I may not be so well known, so here are some good tips on how to prepare me.

Artichocke Salad

4 Servings

4 large artichokes

Juice of ½ lemon

2 tbsp. olive oil

Salt to taste

3 tbsp. chopped parsley

Pepper to taste, freshly ground

Preparation time:

Approx. 20 min.

Serving suggestion:
This less-known dish is great as an appetizer or salad.
Add olives and capers if you like.

1 Cut stems from artichokes. Pull off the tough leaves and cut tips.

2 Place artichokes immediately in water with lemon juice to avoid discoloration.

3 Cut artichokes in half and remove fuzzy center. (the choke)

4 Cut into very thin slices. Mix them with olive oil, salt, pepper and freshly chopped parsley.

Stuffed Artichokes

8 artichokes

Juice of 2 lemons

3 cloves garlic

Olive oil

2 tbsp. fresh parsley or mint, chopped

1½ c. dry bread crumbs (150 g)

2 oz. pitted black olives (80 g)

Salt to taste

Pepper, freshly ground

Preparation time:

Approx. 60 min.
Preheat oven 350°F (180°C)

Serving suggestion:
Serve with saffron-rice or potatoes cooked in their jackets, breaded vegetables or eggplant.

Tip:
To keep the artichokes fresh, put them with the stem in a glass of water, like flowers.

1 Cut artichoke stems, leaving 1½ in. (2½ cm), and pull off the tough leaves. Cut off artichoke top.

2 Leave artichoke whole, use spoon to remove fuzzy centers.

3 To avoid discoloration, put immediately into lemon juice water.

4 Stuffing: Finely chop garlic and olives. Mix with bread crumbs, parsley, salt, pepper and olive oil.

5 Salt artichokes in centers and between leaves. Fill carefully with the breadcrumb mixture and press leaves together.

6 Heat oil in baking dish and place artichokes close together, stems up. Add water ¾ in. (2 cm) deep around the artichokes. Bake 30 min. Baste frequently with liquid.

Pasta with Artichokes

4 - 6 Servings

14 oz. pasta or
spaghetti (400 g)

12 small artichokes (or 6 large)

4 medium tomatoes

1 medium onion

1 small carrot

Pepper to taste, freshly ground

1 clove garlic

1 tsp. salt or to taste

Juice of 1 lemon

2 tbsp. olive oil

Fresh thyme leaves

Preparation time:

Approx. 45 min.

Serving suggestion:
Serve with dry white wine.

Variation:
Add 2 tbsp. pesto to
tomato sauce

1 Cut off stems, pull off tough leaves, cut off tips. Remove fuzzy centers. Cut artichokes in quarters and immediately put in water with lemon juice.

2 Put artichokes in a pan, add lemon water till barely covered. Add salt, cook 15 min.

3 Peel and chop onion, garlic and carrot. Dice tomatoes.

4 Sauté onion and garlic in oil until translucent. Add carrot and cook approx. 10 min.

5 Meanwhile, cook pasta in boiling water until "al dente".

6 Add tomatoes to the pan of onion, garlic and carrot. Cook 10 min. Season with salt and pepper. Add cooked artichoke and mix well. Arrange pasta on plates and top with vegetable sauce. Garnish with fresh thyme leaves.

Eggplant

My delicate flavor is incomparable. My many friends know what's good! Whether fried, baked or combined with other vegetables, I always bring something special to the table.

I love the sun and the warmth that let me grow and ripen. The earth gave me the minerals for your body and I pass these on to you.

»The sun gave me its strength, which I pass on to you!«

Breaded Eggplant

4 Servings

2 medium eggplants (1 kg)

4 heaping tbsp. flour

7 oz. cold water (200 ml)

1½ c. bread crumbs (150 g)

Salt

Pepper

½ c. vegetable oil for frying (125 ml)

Small fresh basil leaves for garnish

Preparation time:

Approx. 35 min.

Serving suggestion:
Serve with vegan garlic dip.

1 Cut eggplant lengthwise into ²/₃ in. slices (1,5 cm). Sprinkle slices on both sides with salt and let stand 20 min.

2 For the batter, whisk flour in water until smooth. Season with salt and pepper.

3 Dab moisture from eggplant slices. Turn slices in flour, then in batter and finally in bread crumbs.

4 Heat oil in frying pan. Fry eggplant slices until golden brown. For a crispy coating, repeat coating procedure before frying.

Stuffed Eggplant

4 Servings

2 large eggplants, approx.
12 oz. each (350 g each)

2 onions

2 green bell peppers

1 red bell pepper

1 clove garlic

3 large tomatoes

1½ oz. pine nuts (40 g)

Dash pepper, freshly ground

Salt to taste

⅛ tbsp. cayenne pepper

1 tbsp. chopped parsley

5 tbsp. olive oil

Chopped oregano

4 tbsp. margarine

1 c. vegetable broth (250 ml)

Preparation time:

Approx. 1½ hours
Preheat oven 400°F (200°C)

Serving suggestion:
With rice, noodles or
boiled potatoes.

1 Cook whole eggplants in boiling water on high heat 10 min., turning frequently. Remove from water, cut lengthwise in half.

2 Scoop out pulp leaving ⅓ in. shell (1 cm). Cut scooped out pulp into small cubes (1 cm) and set aside.

3 Cut onions into thin rings. Mince garlic. Cut peppers in half, seed and cut in thin strips. Dice tomatoes.

4 Heat oil in frying pan and sauté onions and garlic. Add pepper strips and eggplant cubes and cook 5 min.

5 Season with salt, pepper and oregano. Stir in diced tomatoes and pine nuts. Add parsley last. Fill the eggplant shells.

6 Place filled eggplant halves in a greased baking dish and top with pieces of margarine. Pour vegetable broth around the eggplant and bake 20 min.

Eggplant Fried with Artichokes

4 - 6 Servings

2 small eggplants
1 medium artichoke (200 g)
1 red bell pepper
2 lemons
1 tsp. paprika
Pepper, freshly ground
2 cloves garlic
Salt
1/8 tsp. cayenne pepper
1 tbsp. minced parsley
Olive oil
Fresh coriander leaves
for garnish

Preparation time:

Approx. 1½ hours

Serving suggestion:
A tasty dish as
an appetizer or salad.
Serve with Prosecco
wine.

1 Cut eggplants crosswise into thin slices (½ cm). Salt slices on both sides and let stand 30 min.

2 Remove tough leaves from artichoke and cut off the tip. Remove fuzzy center. Cut artichoke into pieces and set aside in lemon juice water.

3 Dressing: Mix well juice of ½ lemon with paprika, pepper, salt, cayenne pepper and olive oil.

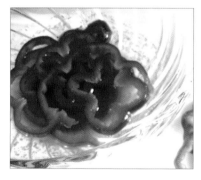

4 Leave bell pepper whole, remove seeds. Cut into thin rings and mix with dressing.

5 Heat oil in frying pan. Dab moisture from eggplant slices and fry in hot oil on both sides until golden brown. Drain well on paper towel.

6 Place artichoke pieces and garlic in pan and fry 8 min., turning several times. Arrange eggplant and artichoke on plates. Top with dressing, sprinkle with minced parsley. Garnish with lemon wedges and coriander leaves.

Cauliflower & Broccoli

We are relatives, and originally came from Asia. We let many florets grow for you. With them you can prepare very tasty dishes containing a lot of folic acid and vitamins. Raw or cooked, as a soup, with rice or noodles – we simply taste delicious. Even children love us!

»We are a rose-greeting from nature for you!«

Rigatoni with Broccoli

4 Servings

11 oz. rigatoni (300 g)

2 medium onions, chopped

2 cloves garlic, minced

2 medium tomatoes, diced

18 oz. broccoli florets (500 g)

2 tbsp. olive oil

Granulated vegetable bouillon

Salt to taste

Pepper to taste, freshly ground

1 tbsp. chopped basil leaves

Pine nuts or sunflower seeds

Preparation time:

Approx. 45 min.

1 Heat oil in frying pan. Peel onions and garlic, finely chop and sauté in hot oil until translucent.

2 Add diced tomatoes, season with vegetable bouillon, salt and pepper. Simmer 15 min. on low heat. Add basil last.

3 Separate broccoli florets and cook 5-8 min. in boiling salted water. Remove from water. Retain water. Gently fold broccoli into tomato sauce.

4 Cook rigatoni "al dente" in the retained water. Drain well and combine with broccoli tomato sauce. Garnish with roasted pine nuts or sunflower seeds (p. 102).

Beer-Batter Cauliflower

4 - 6 Servings

1 cauliflower

1¼ c. beer (300 ml)

1²/₃ c. flour (200 g)

Salt

Pepper, freshly ground

Curry or saffron

Preparation time:

Approx. 40 min.

Serving suggestion:
Serve with your favorite vegan dip.

1 Wash and divide cauliflower into medium size florets.

2 Place in pan, barely cover with water, add salt or vegetable stock and cook approx. 5 min.

3 Beat beer, flour and spices into a smooth batter. Drain cauliflower.

4 Heat oil in a deep-fryer. Dip cauliflower florets, one at a time, in batter and deep fry in hot oil for 2-3 min. until golden brown. Remove from oil and drain.

Cauliflower Salad

4 - 6 Servings

1 cauliflower

1 tbsp. capers

2 tbsp. chopped parsley, thyme and chives

1 tbsp. chopped onion

Vinegar, olive oil

Salt

Pepper, freshly ground

1 Wash and divide cauliflower into very small florets.

2 Combine capers, chopped herbs, onion, olive oil, vinegar, salt and pepper. Add cauliflower. Let stand for a moment.

Fennel

I am a fresh, crunchy bulb and bear in me the power of the earth and of water. My tasty flavor and pleasant aroma refresh you when you prepare me raw; but even when cooked, I taste delicious!

I help your digestion, and with my seeds you can prepare a beneficial tea for your children.

»We give you our freshness!«

Fennel à l'Orange

4 Servings

3 tbsp. margarine

2 onions

2 large or 4 small fennels

2 oranges (organic)

7 oz. orange juice (200 ml)

Pepper

Salt

Granulated vegetable bouillon

Preparation time:

Approx. 30 min.

Serving suggestion:

Serve with rice or small boiled potatoes and a dry white wine.

1 Cut fennels in quarters or halves. Heat 1 tbsp. margarine in frying pan.

2 Sauté finely grated onions. Add fennel and steam.

3 Add orange juice and boil to reduce liquid. Add pepper, salt, vegetable bouillon to taste. Simmer, covered, on low heat 15 min. until tender. Meanwhile, peel and thinly slice oranges.

4 Remove fennel, arrange orange slices on top and keep warm in oven. Boil down remaining liquid by half. Blend in 2 tbsp. margarine with a wire whisk. To serve, pour sauce over fennel and orange slices.

Fennel with Black Olives

4 - 6 Servings

2 lb. fennel (1 kg)
2 medium tomatoes, diced
1 medium onion, chopped
2 cloves garlic, minced
Handful black olives
½ c. dry white wine (125 ml)
6 heaping tbsp. bread crumbs
Granulated vegetable bouillon
Thyme, rosemary
Bay leaf
1 tsp. salt
Pepper to taste, freshly ground
2 tbsp. olive oil
Vegetable shortening

Preparation time:

Approx. 1½ hours
Preheat oven 400°F (200°C)

Serving suggestion:
Serve with noodles, rice or simply fresh, light bread

1 Wash fennel, trim bottoms and stems. Cut into quarters lengthwise. Set green leaves aside.

2 Cook 5 min. in boiling salted water. Remove and drain.

3 Grease baking dish with vegetable shortening, place bay leaf in dish, sprinkle bottom with thyme and rosemary. Arrange fennel pieces in baking dish and season with salt and pepper.

4 Add white wine and bake in oven approx. 10 min.

5 Meanwhile heat pan and quickly fry onions in hot oil. Add tomatoes and minced garlic. Simmer 1 min. Sprinkle granulated vegetable bouillon over baked fennel and scatter black olives on top.

6 Top with a mixture of bread crumbs and finely chopped fennel greens. Bake another 15-20 min. While baking, add wine as needed.

»The kindness of pure nature is our life.«

Grains

*W*e are small, but our small seeds bear a wonderful power! It is this power which we are glad to give you, not only in bread, but also in many other dishes. When you prepare them with love, these dishes will keep the force of the sun and of the earth. The rain gave us to drink; the wind stroked our heads and dried us again. And many micro-organisms helped us grow, because we come from a good soil, withouth solid or liquid manure, without sewage sludge or chemicals. Think of this when you prepare us!

Sunflower Seed Patties

4 Servings

3 medium onions

1 c. sunflower seeds (130 g)

2¹⁄₈ c. water (500 ml)

Handful of dry white bread cubes

1 red bell pepper, diced

1 clove garlic, minced

½ tsp. marjoram, or to taste

2 tsp. granulated vegetable bouillon

Bread crumbs

Frying oil

Salt to taste

Pepper to taste, freshly ground

1 tbsp. chopped parsley

Preparation time:

Approx. 60 min.

1 Peel, finely chop and sauté onions in 2 tbsp. oil. Coarsely chop sunflower seeds in blender and sauté with onions.

2 Season with salt, vegetable bouillon, pepper and marjoram to taste. Add water and bring to a boil.

3 Put all ingredients in a bowl. Mix with bread cubes, garlic, parsley and diced bell pepper. Let stand 15 min.

4 Heat ¼ in. oil in frying pan. Add bread crumbs as needed to form light patties. Fry until crispy brown.

Sunflower Seed Dumplings

4 Servings

3 medium onions

1 c. sunflower seeds (130 g)

2¹/₈ c. water (500 ml)

Handful of dry white bread cubes

1 red bell pepper, diced

1 tbsp. chopped marjoram

2 tsp. granulated vegetable bouillon

Bread crumbs

Frying oil

Salt to taste

Pepper to taste, freshly ground

1 tbsp. chopped parsley

Vegetable broth

Preparation time:

Approx. 60 min.

4 - 6 Servings

Dry bread or rolls

Sunflower seed oil

Preparation time:

Approx. 20 min.

1 Peel, finely chop and sauté onions in 2 tbsp. oil. Coarsely chop sunflower seeds in blender and sauté with onions.

2 Season with salt, vegetable bouillon, pepper and marjoram. Add water and bring to a boil.

3 Put all ingredients into a bowl. Mix with bread cubes, chopped parsley and bell pepper. Let stand 15 min. Add enough bread crumbs to knead into a dough.

4 Form dough into small balls and cook 15 min. in hot, but not boiling, vegetable broth. Delicious with a vegetable sauce (e.g., carrot sauce on p. 68) and rice.

Croutons

1 Cut bread into small cubes (1 cm).

2 Toast in sunflower seed oil until golden brown. Use on noodles, in soups and salads.

Bread Patties

4 - 6 Servings

4 rolls, day-old

1 medium onion

1 c. water (250 ml)

4 tbsp. bread crumbs

1 tbsp. marjoram

1 tbsp. chopped parsley

Dash of nutmeg

Pepper to taste, freshly ground

Salt to taste

5 tbsp. sesame seeds

Frying oil

Preparation time:

Approx. 60 min.

Variation:

Instead of parsley and marjoram choose other herbs, like chives, basil, thyme, lovage ...

Serving suggestion:

Serve with steamed vegetables and your favorite vegan mayonnaise sauce.

1 Cut rolls into small cubes. Peel and finely chop onion.

2 Soak cubed rolls in water. Season with salt, pepper and nutmeg. Add bread crumbs to make a soft dough.

3 Mix onion, marjoram and parsley with dough. Let stand 10 min.

4 Form into patties.

5 Coat patties on all sides with sesame seeds.

6 Heat ¼ in. oil in a frying pan and fry patties until golden brown.

Barley Soup

4 - 6 Servings

2/3 c. pearl barley (120 g)

1 onion

1 carrot

1 leek

4-5 c. vegetable broth
(1 to 1.2 l)

¾ oz. dried or 7 oz. fresh
Porcini mushrooms (20 g dried
or 200 g fresh)

1½ tbsp. margarine

Pepper, freshly ground

Salt to taste

1 tbsp. chopped parsley

Oat milk

Preparation time:

Approx. 60 min.
Soak pearl barley overnight
in water.

Serving suggestion:
This nutritious soup
can be served with coarse
brown bread.

1 Soak barley in water to cover overnight. Drain. Cook barley in a pan of lightly salted water approx. 15 min. Set aside.

2 Soak dried mushrooms in cold water 20 min. Drain well and finely chop. If you are using fresh mushrooms, clean them well and chop.

3 Peel onion and carrot and finely chop. Clean leek and cut into thin rings.

4 Melt margarine in a large pan. Add onion, carrot and leek and sauté. Add musrooms and sauté 5 min. longer.

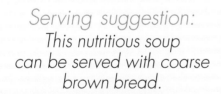

5 Drain cooked barley, add, and sauté briefly.

6 Add vegetable broth and simmer for about 30 min., until barley is tender. Season with salt and pepper. Sprinkle with parsley. If desired, add oat milk.

Millet Risotto with Vegetable Strips

4 - 6 Servings

1 c. millet

2 onions

3-4 carrots

1 oz. parsley root (30 g)

2½ c. vegetable broth (600 ml)

2-3 medium zucchini

1 lb. celery (450 g)

4-5 tomatoes

1 clove garlic

Pepper, freshly ground

½ tsp. salt

6 tbsp. olive oil

1 tbsp. thyme, or to taste

Preparation time:

Approx. 60 min.

1 Chop 1 onion, 1 carrot and parsley root. Sauté in 2 tbsp. oil.

2 Add millet and cook briefly.

3 Add vegetable broth and bring to a boil. Season with salt and pepper. Simmer covered on low heat 25 min.

4 Wash and dice tomatoes. Finely chop garlic and remaining onion and sauté in 2 tbsp. oil until translucent. Add tomatoes and cook 5 min. Season with thyme.

5 Peel remaining carrots, clean zucchini and celery. Cut vegetables lengthwise in very thin strips (1 mm). Cut these strips in half.

6 Fry the carrot strips in another frying pan in 2 tbsp. hot oil for 1 min. Add zucchini and celery and cook for another 5 min. Serve vegetable strips with tomato sauce, and serve millet risotto separately.

Semolina Medallions with Herbs

4 - 6 Servings

2¹/₈ c. water

Salt

1 c. semolina (150 g)

½ c. margarine (100 g)

1 clove garlic

2 tbsp. chopped herbs
(e.g., sage, rosemary)

Pepper, freshly ground

Dash nutmeg

Tomato sauce:

4 ripe tomatoes

2 onions

1 clove garlic

5 tbsp. olive oil

½ tsp. salt

Pepper to taste, freshly ground

Granulated vegetable bouillon

Preparation time:

Approx. 60 min.

Preheat oven 428°F (220°C)

Variation:

Instead of semolina, cornmeal may be used. Enhance tomato sauce with a dash of hot sauce!

1 Bring water and salt to a boil. Add semolina slowly, stirring briskly to avoid lumps. Simmer on low heat 20 min., stirring occasionally.

2 Season with salt, pepper and nutmeg. Spread about ¹/₃ in. thick (1 cm) on a wet board. Let cool.

3 Tomato sauce: Finely chop onions and garlic and dice tomatoes. Sauté onions and garlic in the olive oil until translucent.

4 Add tomatoes. Cover and simmer about 20 min. Season with salt, pepper and granulated vegetable bouillon. Serve tomato sauce separately.

5 Cut cooled semolina into rounds with biscuit cutter or glass. Place semolina rounds like roof tiles in a greased baking dish.

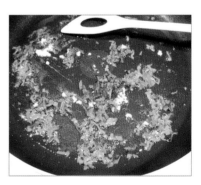

6 Melt margarine in pan and sauté chopped herbs and minced garlic. Sprinkle over the semolina rounds. Bake in oven about 10 min.

Cucumbers

We, too, are children of the sun from the garden of peaceable nature! We are crisp and fresh, grown without solid or liquid manure, sewage sludge or chemicals. Therefore, we are rich in vitamins and minerals. You can prepare a salad from us on a hot summer day; as sweet and sour pickles we enrich many dishes; but we also taste excellent braised and stuffed.

»We offer you our freshness!«

Cucumbers with Tomatoes

4 Servings

2-3 cucumbers

2 onions

½ c. white wine or apple juice (125 ml)

3 medium tomatoes

2 tbsp. olive oil

1 tsp. paprika

Salt to taste

Dash pepper, freshly ground

1 tbsp. chopped fresh dill

Preparation time:

Approx. 40 min.

Serving suggestion:
Serve with rice or parsley potatoes and a fresh salad.

1 Peel cucumbers and cut in half lengthwise, and again cut into 1½ in. pieces (4 cm) and ⅓ in. (1cm) thick.

2 Peel onions and cut into eighths. Heat oil in pan and sauté onions.

3 Add cucumber pieces and sauté briefly. Add white wine. Season with salt, pepper and paprika and simmer 15 min.

4 Cut tomatoes in quarters or eighths and remove seeds. Add to the cucumbers, mix well and steam 5 min. Flavor with fresh dill.

Tip:
The Animal Friendly Cookbook
recommends adding some egg-free
mayonnaise.

Stuffed Cucumbers

4 Servings

2 salad cucumbers

1 onion

$2/3$ c. water (150 ml)

1 tbsp. vinegar

½ c. sunflower seeds (70 g)

1 clove garlic

2 tbsp. margarine

Salt to taste

Pepper to taste, freshly ground

Preparation time:

Approx. 1½ hours

Serving suggestion:

**As appetizers on
a cold buffet**

1 Clean cucumbers well, cut at an angle crosswise into 1½ in. (4 cm) slices and hollow out the centers.

2 Chop sunflower seeds in blender. Peel and finely chop onion and garlic. Mince the cucumber pulp that was hollowed out.

3 In a small pan, bring to boil water, vinegar, sunflower seeds, garlic, salt and pepper. Remove from heat and let soak 10 min.

4 Blend sunflower seeds with onion, cucumber pulp and margarine into a fine pureé. Stuff cucumber slices with this filling. Serve chilled.

Cucumber Cocktail

4 Servings

2 salad cucumbers

1 clove garlic

1 onion

Juice of 1 lemon

Salt to taste

1 tbsp. olive oil

Dash pepper, freshly ground

2 tsp. fresh dill

1 Peel cucumbers and finely grate. Peel and crush garlic. Peel onion and finely chop.

2 Combine lemon juice and all other ingredients in a blender. Blend until smooth. Serve chilled in glasses with a slice of lemon.

Hokkaido Squash

»I live!«

Hokkaido is a winter squash not readily available in the U.S. Other winter squash like butternut, acorn or delicata are great substitutes. A special feature of the Hokkaido squash is that the rind can also be cooked and used along with the pulp. If you substitute other squash types however, please first remove the rind.

As you can see, I am brimming with sunlight, healthy life energy and joy of living. With me you can cook delicious meals such as tasty soups or vegetable casseroles – and so much more. I had the chance to grow in peaceable cultivation. That's why I taste especially good!

Hokkaido Soup

4 - 6 Servings

3¼ lb. Hokkaido squash or Butternut (1.5 kg)

2 medium onions, chopped

4¼ c. water (1 l)

2-4 c. oat milk or water (½ - 1 l)

2 tbsp. sunflower oil

2 tbsp. granulated vegetable bouillon

Salt, freshly ground pepper to taste

Dash nutmeg

Preparation time:

Approx. 45 min.

Serving suggestion: Also delicious as a curry dish: Add 1-2 tbsp. curry powder, enhanced with whipped coconut milk.

1 Wash the Hokkaido, cut out spots, leave rind intact. Other squash types should have rind removed. Remove seeds with spoon.

2 Cut into cubes. Chop onions.

3 Sauté onions in sunflower oil, add Hokkaido cubes and continue to sauté. Cover with water and cook until the Hokkaido falls apart.

4 Pureé with a mixer. Add oat milk as needed for creamy consistency. Season with vegetable bouillon, salt, pepper and nutmeg.

Hokkaido Gnocchi

4 - 6 Servings

2 lb. Hokkaido squash (1 kg)

Water

4-5 large potatoes (1 kg)

$1^2/_3$ c. flour (200 g)

Salt to taste

Dash nutmeg

5 sage leaves, fresh

5 tbsp. olive oil

Preparation time:

Approx. 60 min.
Preheat oven 338°F (170°C)

Serving suggestion:
Serve with a large Italian salad and Chianti wine or fruit juice of your choice.

1 Clean Hokkaido well, cut in half.Scrape out seeds and cut in slices. Bake in oven about 30 min.

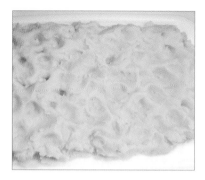

2 Boil unpeeled potatoes until tender, about 30 min. Peel and mash. Spread out on board to cool.

3 Pureé Hokkaido and let cool. Mix with potatoes and season with salt and nutmeg. Make into dough using flour as needed to keep dough from sticking when kneading.

4 Shape dough into thin rolls and cut diagonally into small "gnocchi".

5 Cook gnocchi in rapidly boiling salted water until they rise to the surface. Carefully lift out of water with slotted spoon.

6 Heat oil and sage leaves in a frying pan. Stir in the gnocchi and briefly sauté. Serve at once.

Note:
The original recipe calls for
parmesan cheese.
The Animal Friendly Cookbook
suggests using toasted almonds
or pine nuts instead.

Hokkaido Fritters

4 - 6 Servings

2 lb. Hokkaido squash (1 kg)

2-3 tbsp. flour

Dash nutmeg

Salt

Pepper to taste, freshly ground

Frying oil

Preparation time.

Approx. 30 min.

1 Clean Hokkaido, remove seeds and coarsely grate pulp.

2 Season grated pulp with salt, pepper and nutmeg and let stand for 10 min.

3 Sprinkle with flour until the grated pulp holds together to form loose patties.

4 Deep fry patties in ¼ in. hot oil (365°F) until crisp.

Baked Hokkaido Slices

4 - 6 Servings

1 large Hokkaido squash

2 tsp. rosemary

2 tbsp. olive oil

Salt

Pepper to taste, freshly ground

Preparation time:

Approx. 30 min.

Preheat oven 428°F (220°C)

1 Wash Hokkaido and cut out spots. Cut in half and scrape out seeds and fibers. Cut in slices and place on a baking sheet.

2 Sprinkle with olive oil, season well with salt, pepper and rosemary. Bake in oven until tender, about 20 min.

Hokkaido Salad

4 - 6 Servings

1½ lb. Hokkaido squash
(700 g)

1 medium onion

½ green bell pepper

1 tbsp. mustard, medium hot

Salt

Pepper to taste, freshly ground

2 tbsp. olive oil

2 tbsp. water

Preparation time:

Approx. 30 min.

1 Clean, remove seeds and dice Hokkaido.

2 Cook in boiling, salted water 5 min. Drain and let cool.

3 Finely chop onion, cut green pepper into thin strips and add to Hokkaido.

4 Dressing: Mix well using fork or mixer: mustard, olive oil, water, salt and pepper. Pour over salad.

Hokkaido-Mashed Potatoes

4 - 6 Servings

1 large Hokkaido squash

4 medium potatoes (500 g)

1½ c. oat milk (300 g)

Dash nutmeg

Salt

Pepper to taste, freshly ground

Preparation time:

Approx. 45 min.
Preheat oven 400°F (200°C)

1 Clean and core Hokkaido. Cut in slices and place on baking sheet. Bake in oven until tender, approx. 20 min.

2 Cook unpeeled potatoes until tender. Peel and mash with cooked Hokkaido. Season to taste. Heat oak milk and add. Stir well and heat briefly.

The Animal Friendly Cookbook recommends enhancing the Hokkaido salad with a spoonful of egg-free mayonnaise.

Hokkaido Creme

4 - 6 Servings

2 lb. Hokkaido
(or Butternut) squash (1 kg)

1 qt. water (1 l)

1 tsp. cinnamon

8 tbsp. sugar (100 g)

$1/8$ tsp. vanilla powder or
½ tsp. vanilla flavoring

Kiwi or other fruits to garnish

Preparation time:

Overnight
Approx. 30 min, before and
after overnight

Serving suggestion:
Serve with coconut vanilla
sauce on p. 18.

Variation:
You can also prepare
this recipe using edible
chestnuts.

1 Clean and core Hokkaido and cut into large cubes.

2 Cook in water until fork-tender.

3 Drain well. Pureé in a bowl with electrix mixer.

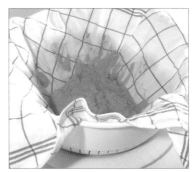

4 Place the pureé in a clean dishtowel and drain overnight. Next day mix well with cinnamon, sugar and vanilla.

5 Press through a ricer, directly onto dessert dishes, to make thin "spaghetti".

6 Garnish with fruit and cookies.

Carrots

Experience all the good things that I contain! The many vitamins give your eyes a sparkle and many minerals strengthen your body. I smile at you with my cheerful color and give you joy in many dishes, raw or cooked, as an appetizer, soup, casserole, salad or even sweetened. For small children I am often pureed. I am easy to digest and healthy, especially when I have the chance to grow and ripen in a natural way through peaceable cultivation.

»I put a sparkle in your eyes!«

Fine Carrot Soup

4 - 6 Servings

3-4 medium carrots (500 g)

3 medium onions

3$^1/_3$ c. vegetable broth (800 ml)

3 tbsp. margarine

Juice and grated peel of 1 orange (organic)

Oat milk

Salt

Pepper to taste, freshly ground

Fresh mint leaves for garnish

Preparation time:

Approx. 45 min.

1 Cut onions into rings. Sauté onions in margarine until translucent.

2 Cut carrots into pieces, and sauté with the onions.

3 Add vegetable broth and simmer covered on low heat about 15 min. Add orange juice and grated peel.

4 Blend well in mixer. Add oat milk as needed for a creamy consistency. Season with salt and pepper. Garnish with minced mint leaves (mixed in oat milk).

Carrot-Onion Sauce

4 - 6 Servings

2-3 carrots

2 medium onions

2 tomatoes

1 red bell pepper

3 tbsp. flour

½ c. red wine or apple juice
(100 ml)

¾ c. water (200 ml)

Salt

Pepper to taste, freshly ground

2 tsp. granulated vegetable
bouillon

Oil

Preparation time:

Approx. 45 min.

Serving suggestion:
Delicious with vegetarian
patties (pp. 40, 44) and rice.

1 Peel onions, finely chop and sauté in pan with 2 tbsp. oil.

2 Clean carrots, cut into thin slices and sauté with onions. Add finely chopped tomatoes and bell pepper.

3 Sauté approx. 5 min. Sprinkle with flour, sauté until flour is brown. Stir in wine or apple juice. Add water and bring to a boil, stirring constantly.

4 Season with pepper, salt and vegetable bouillon. Simmer on low heat until tender. Press through sieve or blend in a mixer to make a sauce.

Carrot and Raisin Salad

4 - 6 Servings

3-4 medium carrots

2 tbsp. raisins

1 c. orange juice

Juice of 1 lemon

1 tsp. granulated vegetable
bouillon

A few walnuts

Preparation time:

Approx. 20 min.

1 Mix lemon juice, orange juice, vegetable bouillon and raisins.

2 Peel carrots and grate them directly into the dressing so they do not turn brown. Top with coarsely chopped walnuts.

Potatoes

I carry within the joy and life-force that comes from a healthy, happy soil, and I pass these on to you. With many other kinds of vegetables, I can be prepared as a salad, croquettes, mashed, or as hash browns, as well as a soup, stew, au gratin and many more dishes. I'm a favorite among children and adults! Since I come from peaceable cultivation, I am healthy and am able to give you many vitamins and minerals!

»*We are good and give you only the best.*«

Vegetarian Moussake

4 Servings

2½ c. mashed potatoes (600 g)

1 red bell pepper

1 green bell pepper

2 small onions

1 eggplant

4 tomatoes

2 cloves garlic

4 tbsp. bread crumbs

Salt

Pepper to taste, freshly ground

1 tbsp. chopped parsley

Olive oil

Preparation time:

Approx. 30 min.
Preheat oven 482°F (250°C)

1 Heat oil in pan. Finely chop onions, mince garlic and sauté in hot oil.

2 Dice eggplant, peppers and tomatoes, add to onion and garlic and sauté.

3 Grease a casserole dish and cover bottom with half of the sautéed vegetables. Spread mashed potatoes on top (thicker at the edges).

4 Cover with remaining vegetables and sprinkle with a mixture of bread crumbs, parsley, garlic and 1 tbsp. oil. Bake briefly in oven.

Stuffed Baked Potatoes

4 - 6 Servings

4-6 large potatoes

1 red bell pepper

1 green bell pepper

1 small onion

3 tomatoes

1 clove garlic

4 tsp. paprika

½ tsp. ground caraway seeds

Salt

Pepper to taste, freshly ground

Olive oil

1 tsp. marjoram

Preparation time:

Approx. 1½ hours
Preheat oven 400°F (200°C)

Serving suggestion:

Serve with a spoonful of egg-free mayonnaise and a fresh salad.

Variation:

Using a small spoon or a deco-pastry bag, fill the hollowed-out potato with a vegan sauce of your choice and bake an additional 5 min. at 375°F (180°C)

1 Wash potatoes well, wrap in foil. Bake approx. one hour in preheated oven.

2 Finely chop onion and mince garlic. Dice peppers and tomatoes.

3 Heat oil in pan. Sauté onion and garlic in hot oil. Add peppers and sauté 5 min. Add tomatoes and cook for 2 min. Add seasoning and marjoram.

4 Remove potatoes from oven. Cut a "lid" lengthwise one third from top. Hollow out bottoms leaving ¼ in. (4 mm) on the bottom and sides.

5 Cut potato pulp and lids into small cubes. Fold into pepper-tomato mixture. Season with salt and pepper.

6 Fill hollowed potatoes with this mixture. Bake briefly and serve hot.

Potato Salad with Ripe Olives

4 - 6 Servings

4-5 medium potatoes

2 medium onions

1 clove garlic

2 tbsp. capers

3 oz. black olives (80 g)

8 tbsp. olive oil

2 tbsp. white-wine vinegar

Pinch of sugar

1 tbsp. chopped parsley

Salt

Pepper to taste, freshly ground

Preparation time:

Approx. 45 min.

1 Cook washed potatoes in lightly salted water 20 min. until tender but firm.

2 Cut onions in thin rings. Heat vinegar and sugar in pan, add onions and simmer on low heat 5 min.

3 In a bowl combine minced garlic, capers, olives and onions with liquid. Mix well with salt, pepper and olive oil.

4 While still warm, peel and thinly slice potatoes (ca. 3 mm). Fold in with other ingredients and let stand 10 min. Sprinkle with chopped parsley.

Potato Salad

4 - 6 Servings

4-5 potatoes (800 g)

3 dill pickles

1 onion, finely chopped

2 tbsp. chopped chives

Olive oil, vinegar

Salt

Pepper to taste, freshly ground

Preparation time:

Approx. 45 min.

1 Cook potatoes in water until tender, but firm. Drain, peel and thinly slice (3 mm thick). Dice pickles.

2 In a bowl, carefully fold still warm potato slices with pickles and onion. Season with salt, pepper, oil and vinegar. Garnish with chives.

Potato Croquettes

4 - 6 Servings

2½ c. mashed potatoes
(day old is best)

2 tbsp. chopped parsley
or chives

6 tbsp. flour

Bread crumbs

Frying oil

7 oz. water (200 ml)

Preparation time:

Approx. 30 min.

Serving suggestion:
Goes well with vegetables
or a fresh salad such as
arugula and tomato.
Enhance with a hearty
vegan dip of your choice.

1 Mix mashed potatoes with chopped parsley. If not firm enough, add 2 tbsp. flour.

2 For the coating: Mix 4 heaping tbsp. flour with water until smooth.

3 With wet hands shape mashed potatoes into croquettes. Dip croquettes into coating and roll in bread crumbs.

4 Heat ¼ in. oil in pan. Fry croquettes in hot oil until crisp.

Mashed Potatoes

4 - 6 Servings

4-5 large potatoes

1¼ c. oat milk

4 tbsp. margarine

Pinch nutmeg

Salt

Pepper to taste, freshly ground

Preparation time:

Approx. 40 min.

1 Boil unpeeled potatoes approx. 30 min. Peel and mash with potato masher or put through ricer directly into pan.

2 Heat margarine with oat milk separately, add to potatoes and beat with whisk until creamy. Flavor with nutmeg, salt and pepper. Heat again, stirring constantly. Serve at once.

Potatoes-Gratin

4 - 6 Servings

4 medium boiled potatoes
(day old is best)

¾ c. béchamel sauce (p. 54)
flavored with your favorite herbs

¾ c. water (180 ml)

2 tbsp. white wine

2 tbsp. chopped parsley

1 tbsp. margarine

Preparation time:

Approx. 45 min.
Preheat oven 375°F (190°C)

Variation:
Try 1-2 tbsp. pesto sauce
mixed in water.

1 Peel boiled potatoes and cut into thin (4 mm) slices.

2 Using a wire whisk, blend béchamel sauce with your favorite herbs, water and white wine.

3 Grease shallow casserole dish with margarine and place sliced potatoes like roofing tiles in the dish. Pour cream mixture evenly over potato slices.

4 Bake approx. 20 min. until top is lightly brown. Garnish with chopped parsley.

Potato-Garlic Soup

4 - 6 Servings

4 medium potatoes

1 large onion

1 handful wild garlic, chopped
(or 2 cloves garlic, crushed)

Fresh herbs: parsley, basil, dill

2 tbsp. granulated vegetable
bouillon

3¾ c. water (750 ml)

4 - 6 tbsp. olive oil

Salt

1 Peel potatoes and onion. Dice small. Add to heated olive oil in frying pan with chopped wild garlic or crushed garlic and sauté briefly. Pour in water and cook approx. 20 min.

2 Season to taste with bouillon and salt. Add fresh herbs finely chopped and pureé with wand-mixer. To thin, add hot water.

Swiss Rösti

4 - 6 Servings

5 large potatoes, unpeeled
(preferably boiled day before)

2 tbsp. oil or margarine

Salt and freshly ground pepper,
to taste

Preparation time:

Approx. 25 min.

Variation:
Add minced wild garlic
mixed with olive oil directly
into potato mixture before
frying.

1 Boil unpeeled potatoes approx. 30 min. until tender. Set aside overnight.

2 Peel and grate potatoes. Season with salt and pepper.

3 Heat oil in frying pan. Add potatoes and shape a "Rösti" (flat round form). Cook on medium heat until bottom is golden brown.

4 Turn with the help of a plate and brown the other side. Onion relish (see page 168) and green salad help make a good meal.

Rosemary Potatoes

4 - 6 Servings

2 lb. potatoes (1 kg)

3 cloves garlic, crushed

6 tbsp. olive oil

2 tsp. rosemary

Salt to taste

Preparation time:

Approx. 60 min.
Prehat oven 350°F (175°C)

1 Pour olive oil into large bowl. Add crushed garlic. Peel potatoes, cut in quarters or eighths and mix well with olive oil and garlic. Let stand 5 min.

2 Cover baking sheet with foil and brush with oil. Spread potatoes on foil. Sprinkle with rosemary and salt. Bake in preheated oven 45 min., until crisp.

Tortilla Española

4 Servings

5 large potatoes

2 medium onions

6 tbsp. olive oil

Salt and freshly ground pepper, to taste

3 heaping tbsp. flour

1 ¼ c. water (300ml)

Preparation time:

Approx. 60 min.

Serving suggestion:
Instead of onions, use spinach, bell peppers or other vegetables. Serve with green salad and fresh tomatoes.

1 Peel and slice raw potatoes. Peel onions and finely chop.

2 Heat oil in pan. Sauté onions until translucent. Add potatoes and salt and fry on medium heat. Add water as needed.

3 Meanwhile, cream flour in water until smooth. Season with salt and pepper.

4 When tender, remove potato-onion mixture from pan, drain well, add flour cream and mix well.

5 Heat frying pan with oil, fry single portions, ¹/₃ in. thick (1 cm).

6 When bottom no longer sticks to pan, turn tortilla by using a plate and brown other side.

Cabbage

We come in many varieties and in each of our leaves is hidden a large portion of strength. We give your body lots of Vitamin C and folic acid and a lot of life-energy, especially when we grow in healthy soil with the power of the sun and earth. I bear the life in me and am a true nourishment for life.

»I give you my strength!«

Cabbage Curry

4 Servings

1 small head cabbage

1 large potato

1 large tomato

½ oz. (15 g) fresh ginger root or ¹/₈ tsp. powdered ginger

1 c. coconut milk (250 ml)

3 tbsp. margarine

3 bay leaves

4 tsp. curry

Salt and freshly ground pepper, to taste

1 tsp. sugar

Preparation time:

Approx. 50 min.

1 Quarter cabbage, remove core and shred. Peel and dice potato.

2 Dice tomato. Peel and slice ginger root. Heat margarine in pan and briefly sauté the curry.

3 Add cabbage and potato and fry 3 min, stirring constantly. Season with salt, pepper and sugar.

4 Mix in bay leaves, tomato and ginger. Add coconut milk, cover and simmer on low heat 25 min. Serve with bread.

Potato Fritters with Sauerkraut

4 Servings

For the potato fritters:

4 large potatoes

8 heaping tbsp. flour

½ c. water (100 ml)

Margarine

Salt to taste

For the sauerkraut:

17 oz. sauerkraut (500 g)

1 medium onion

8½ oz. (250 ml) white or sparkling wine, apple juice or mix equal amounts apple juice and water

6½ tbsp. margarine

1 bay leaf

2 tsp. granulated vegetable bouillon

Salt and freshly ground pepper, to taste

Preparation time:

Approx. 60 min.

Variation:

Place salad leaves, onion rings and tomato slices between two fritters.

1 Peel and finely chop onion. Melt half the margarine in a pan, add two-thirds onion and sauté until transparent.

2 Cut sauerkraut into smaller pieces and add to sautéed onion. Add bay leaf, salt and pepper, bouillon and sauté together.

3 Add wine. Reduce heat and cook covered, 30-40 min.

4 Meanwhile, peel potatoes and coarsely grate.

5 Mix grated potatoes, flour, remaining onion, salt and water.

6 Heat margarine in frying pan. Shape potato mixture into 8 fritters and fry until crisp on both sides. Place one fritter on each plate, cover each with about ¼ of the sauerkraut mixture and top with a second fritter.

Red Cabbage and Potatoes Gratin

4 - 6 Servings

2 lb. red cabbage (1 kg)

1 lb. Shiitake mushrooms (500 g)

2 small onions

1 red bell pepper

2 sour apples

½ c. margarine (100 g)

4 tbsp. wine vinegar

3-4 medium potatoes

4½ oz. white wine or apple juice (125 ml)

4½ oz. vegetable broth (125 ml)

Salt and freshly ground pepper, to taste

1 tbsp. chopped lovage (parsley family)

Preparation time:

Approx. 1½ hours
Preheat oven 400°F (200°C)

Serving suggestion:
Serve with fresh dark bread, a winter salad and red wine.

1 Clean shiitake mushrooms, cut into pieces if necessary. Sauté briefly in margarine. Set aside.

2 Clean cabbage, cut in half, remove core and shred. Clean and finely chop bell pepper. Cut apples in fourths with skin, core and chop.

3 Peel and dice onions. Melt margarine in a saucepan, add chopped onions and sauté briefly. Add chopped pepper and apples; sauté 5 min. longer.

4 Add shredded cabbage and wine-vinegar, cover and simmer approx. 30 min. Season with salt and pepper.

5 Place cabbage mixture in greased baking dish. Spread mushrooms on top. Peel potatoes, thinly slice and arrange like roof tiles over mushrooms and cabbage.

6 Bake 15. min. Mix wine or apple juice and vegetable broth and pour over. Sprinkle with pepper and bake another 35-40 min. Garnish with chopped lovage and serve.

Savoy Cabbage Rolls

1 head Savoy cabbage

1 ½ c. sunflower seeds (200 g)

2 large onions

2 green bell peppers

2 fresh tomatoes

Salt and freshly ground pepper,
to taste

½ c. water (125 ml)

Oil

Preparation time:

Approx. 45 min.
Preheat oven 300°F (150°C)

Serving suggestion:

Serve with potatoes,
boiled in their skins.
Garnish with toasted
bread crumbs and
sautéed, cubed bell
peppers.
Serve with tomato sauce.

1 Clean cabbage and cook whole in salted walter until outer leaves are tender, approx. 5 min.

2 Remove cabbage from water. Cut single leaves from head. If not tender, briefly cook again in salted water.

3 Filling: Heat oil in pan; finely chop onions and sauté until translucent.

4 Coarsely chop sunflower seeds in a blender and add to onions. Clean and dice tomatoes and peppers, sauté with onions. Add water and simmer 10 min.

5 Place 1 tbsp. filling on each cabbage leaf. Fold in the ends of the leaves.

6 Roll around the filling. Place cabbage rolls in a greased, ovenproof dish. Bake approx. 30 min.

Leeks

I am a relative of the onion, but finer and milder in flavor. I activate many cleansing functions in your body. I do not like to be alone. Therefore you find me on your plate mostly in the company of other vegetables, in various combinations. I enrich and round off the flavor in soups, gratins, mashed potatoes, casseroles and many other dishes. You can also find me raw in salads – tasty, fortifying and healthy. I am a versatile ingredient of delicious cooking.

»I am tasty, strong and healthy.«

Leek Soup

4 Servings

½ lb. leeks (250 g)

1 carrot

1 stalk celery (ca. 40 g)

⅔ c. oat milk (150 ml)

4¼ c. vegetable broth (1 l)

6½ tbsp. margarine

¼ c. flour (30 g)

Dash freshly grated nutmeg

Salt and freshly ground pepper, to taste

1 tbsp. chopped parsley

2 bay leaves

Preparation time:

Approx. 40 min.

Variation:

For a hearty flavor, add 2 tbsp. chopped wild garlic.

1 Clean and finely chop leeks, using the dark green stalks. Clean and finely chop celery and carrot.

2 Melt half the margarine in a pan. Add leeks, carrot, celery and sauté. Sprinkle with flour, stir and sauté another 1-2 min.

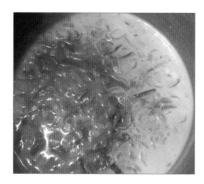

3 Add vegetable broth, stir until smooth. Add bay leaves. Bring to a boil, reduce heat and simmer 20 min. Remove bay leaves.

4 Stir in oat milk. Season with salt, pepper and nutmeg. Pureé soup in blender. Add remaining margarine and sprinkle with parsley.

Leek Gratin

4 - 6 Servings

2½ lb. leeks (1.2 kg)

2 tbsp. flour

1 tbsp. paprika

2 tbsp. margarine

1 tbsp. flour

3 tbsp. chopped parsley

1 red bell pepper

For the Béchamel sauce:

4 tbsp. margarine

2/3 c. preheated oat milk (150 ml)

Salt and freshly ground pepper, to taste

¼ tsp. nutmeg

2 tsp. granulated vegetable bouillon

Preparation time:

Approx. 45 min.
Preheat oven 400°F (200°C)

Serving suggestion:
Serve with boiled potatoes or rice.

1 Cut roots and dark green stalks from leeks (the green stalks can be used in soup).

2 Wash leeks thoroughly. Along length of leeks, make shallow diagonal cuts about every ¾ in. (2 cm). Cook in salted water 15 min. Clean and dice pepper.

3 Béchamel sauce: Melt margarine in pan. Add flour and cook briefly.

4 Slowly add preheated oat milk, stirring constantly. Season well with salt, nutmeg and vegetable bouillon. Bring to a boil.

5 Coat leeks in mixture of 2 tbsp. flour and paprika. In large frying pan, melt margarine and sauté leeks until golden brown.

6 Place leeks in a greased oven-proof dish. Pour béchamel sauce on top and season with ground pepper. Bake for 20 min. Sprinkle with parsley and chopped pepper and serve at once.

Leek-Apple Gratin

4 Servings

4 leeks

2 apples (somewhat sour)

4 tbsp. oil

1²/₃ c. oat milk (400 ml)

4 tbsp. flour

²/₃ c. sunflower seeds (80 g)

Dash nutmeg

2 tsp. granulated vegetable bouillon

Salt and freshly ground pepper, to taste

Preparation time:

Approx. 50 min.
Preheat oven 400°F (200°C)

Serving suggestion:
Serve with boiled potatoes or rice.

1 Cut roots and tough green stalks from leeks. Slice leeks into thin rings. Peel apples and coarsely grate.

2 Heat oil in pan. Sauté leeks approx. 8 min. Season with salt and pepper. Mix in grated apples.

3 In a bowl, mix flour and oat milk until smooth. Season well with nutmeg, salt, pepper and vegetable bouillon. Roast sunflower seeds in frying pan without oil.

4 Place leeks-apple mixture in greased baking dish. Sprinkle with sunflower seeds and cover with flour-oat milk sauce. Bake 35 min.

"Leek-Asparagus"

4 Servings

2 large leeks

1 tomato

Salt to taste

2 tbsp. olive oil

1 tbsp. vinegar

Preparation time:

Approx. 30 min.

1 Clean leeks, remove roots and tough green stalks. Cook white stalks in boiling water 15 min.

2 Coat the leek with olive oil, salt and vinegar. Serve cold as salad or appetizer with chopped tomato.

Corn

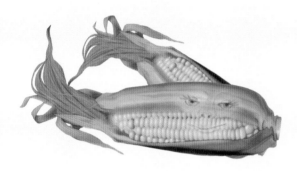

»I am tasty, strong and healthy for you.«

My kernels are soft, juicy and sweet and can be prepared in a variety of ways, like other vegetables, or simply as corn on the cob with margarine and salt. But you can also make cornmeal from me for bread, polenta, corn chips and tortillas. My fresh kernels contain a lot of sugar that transforms into starch when stored, but they also have a lot of minerals and vitamins.

Polenta Stuffed Zucchini

4 Servings

2 Zucchini (each 350 g)

2 oz. fresh Shiitake mushrooms (50 g)

1-2 stalks of celery

1-2 medium carrots

1 small onion

1 clove garlic

2 tbsp. olive oil

¾ c. cornmeal (100 g)

2½ c. vegetable broth (600 ml)

1 tbsp. thyme

1 tsp. rosemary

Salt and freshly ground pepper, to taste

1½ tbsp. margarine

Preparation time:

Approx. 60 min.
Preheat oven 400°F (200°C)

1 Wash zucchini, cut in half lengthwise. Hollow out centers. Leave shell ¼ in. thick. Cut removed pulp into cubes. Clean celery, peel carrots and mince both.

2 Heat oil in a pan and sauté peeled and chopped onion and garlic. Add celery, carrots and zucchini cubes. Stir in cornmeal and toast lightly.

3 Wash and chop mushrooms. Add mushrooms and 1²/₃ c. (400 ml) vegetable broth. Bring to a boil and simmer 15 min. Season with thyme, rosemary, salt and pepper.

4 Lightly salt zucchini halves and fill with cornmeal vegetable mixture. Pour remaining vegetable broth into baking dish. Place filled zucchini halves in dish, dot with margarine. Bake 25 min.

Polenta Squares with Shiitake-Filling

4 - 6 Servings

1 c. cornmeal (150 g)

4¼ c. water (1 l)

½ c. margarine (100 g)

½ lb. fresh Shiitake mushrooms (250 g)

1 small onion

1 clove garlic

Dash nutmeg

1 tbsp. thyme

1 tbsp. chopped parsley

3 tbsp. flour

3 tbsp. olive oil

Salt and freshly ground pepper, to taste

Bread crumbs

Preparation time:

Approx. 45 min.

Serving suggestion:
Serve with tomato sauce made from fresh tomatoes and a salad.

1 Boil 3¼ c. (750 ml) water. Add salt, nutmeg and margarine. Stir in cornmeal using a wire whisk. Simmer on low heat 10 min., stirring constantly.

2 In a greased, shallow baking dish, spread the cooked cornmeal (polenta) approx. ¹/₃ in. thick (1 cm). Let cool.

3 Slice mushrooms coarsely. Peel and finely chop onion and garlic.

4 Melt margarine in frying pan. Add onion and garlic and sauté until translucent. Add mushrooms and sauté. Season with herbs.

5 Cut polenta in rectangles approx. 3 x 4 in. (7 x 10 cm). Spread half the rectangles with mushroom mixture and cover with the other half. Press lightly.

6 Make a batter of 3 tbsp. flour and 1 c. water (250 ml). Dip these filled polenta rectangles in batter and then coat with bread crumbs. Fry in hot oil on both sides until golden brown.

Swiss Chard

Although I am not a relative of spinach, I am often prepared like it. While my leaves are still young and tender they are a delicacy as a salad. But also cooked, my stems and leaves make a very fine dish. I can be used in various ways, alone or with noodles, rice and other vegetables. I give my life's energy to your organs, stimulating their activity.

»I give my life's energy to your organs.«

Swiss Chard

4 Servings

1²/₃ lb. Swiss chard (750 g)

2 tbsp. margarine

1 clove garlic

½ c. white wine (¹/₈ l)

4¼ c. vegetable broth (1 l)

Dash freshly grated nutmeg

Salt and freshly ground pepper, to taste

2 tbsp. toasted sunflower seeds or pine nuts

Preparation time:

Approx. 30 min.

Serving suggestion:
Serve with mashed potatoes and lots of chives, or with rice.

1 Wash Swiss chard and cut ends off stems. Cut leaves from stems into strips and cut both stems and leaf strips into pieces approx. ¹/₃ in. wide (1 cm).

2 Melt margarine in frying pan. Add cut stems, cover and simmer on low heat 8 min. Add white wine and vegetable broth.

3 Add crushed garlic and chard leaves. Season to taste with salt, pepper and nutmeg. Simmer 5 min.

4 Toast sunflower seeds or pine nuts in a dry pan. Sprinkle over cooked Swiss chard and serve.

Stuffed Swiss Chard Leaves

4 - 6 Servings

12 large Swiss chard leaves
2 tbsp. long grain rice
1 small onion
½ c. small dark grapes (60 g)
3 tbsp. olive oil
2 tbsp. margarine
⅓ c. pine nuts (40 g)
½ c. vegetable broth (⅛ l)
1¾ c. bread crumbs (170 g)
Salt and freshly ground pepper,
to taste

Preparation time:

Approx. 60 min.
Preheat oven 400°F (200°C)

Serving suggestion:
Serve with a tomato or carrot sauce. A fresh salad and a dry white wine round off this dish.

1 Carefully wash Swiss chard leaves and blot dry. Remove stems and cut into small pieces.

2 Blanch leaves quickly in boiling water.

3 Cook rice in boiling water 12 min. until half done. Drain in sieve and rinse with cold water. Let stand.

4 Peel onion and finely chop. Heat 1 tbsp. oil in pan and lightly sauté onion with ¼ c. pine nuts (30 g). Add chopped stems and sauté 10 min.

5 Combine onion mixture with rice and grapes. Season with salt and pepper. Melt margarine in pan; add bread crumbs and remaining pine nuts and sauté. Spread Swiss chard leaves and put 1 tbsp. of this mixture on each.

6 Fold in sides and roll into small packages. Place close together in greased baking dish. Pour in vegetable broth and olive oil. Top with the bread crumb pine nut mixture. Bake 30 min.

Crêpes with Swiss Chard Filling

4 - 6 Servings

2 lb. Swiss chard (1 kg)

1 medium onion

1 c. beer or sparkling water (250 ml)

1 c. flour (120 g)

6½ tbsp. margarine

2/3 c. chopped walnuts (80 g)

1 c. oat milk (250 ml)

Dash nutmeg

Salt and freshly ground pepper, to taste

3 tbsp. parsley

1 tsp. oregano

Preparation time:

Approx. 60 min.
Preheat oven 428°F (220°C)

Serving suggestion:
Serve with rice or parsley-potatoes and a fresh tomato salad.

1 For the batter: Beat beer or sparkling water and 7/8 c. flour (100 g) until smooth. Add salt and pepper and let stand 60 min.

2 Meanwhile, finely chop onion and sauté in ¼ c. (50 g) margarine until translucent. Add walnuts and sauté briefly.

3 Clean Swiss chard, chop stems and cut leaves into strips. Add to onions and walnuts. Season with salt, pepper and nutmeg, and cook on low heat 10 min.

4 Melt a little margarine in a pan. Pour in enough batter to thinly cover bottom of pan, and cook on both sides until golden brown. Make 8 crêpes and let cool.

5 For the béchamel sauce: Melt 2 tbsp. margarine, add remaining flour and cook 1-2 min. Heat oat milk and add, beating until smooth. Season with salt, pepper and nutmeg. Let simmer 15 min.

6 Spread filling on crêpes, roll and place close together in a greased baking dish. Pour béchamel sauce over crêpes and bake 10 min. Sprinkle with parsley and oregano.

Pasta

*W*hether short or long, colored or white, we always bring joy to each table. Not only children love us, but adults, as well. And we can be prepared in so many different ways: with all kinds of sauces, in a casserole, or au gratin. Served warm in winter and as a refreshing, cool salad on hot summer days, we are always a suitable, light and enjoyable dish!

Spaghetti with Red Wine Onion Sauce

4 Servings

14 oz. (400 g) spaghetti

1 large onion or scallions

4 tomatoes

8½ oz. dry red wine (250 ml)

1 clove garlic

4 tbsp. olive oil

Salt and freshly ground pepper, to taste

1 tbsp. chopped parsley

Preparation time:

Approx. 40 min.

1 Peel onion and finely chop. Peel and crush garlic. Wash and chop tomatoes.

2 Heat olive oil in a pan and sauté onion and garlic until translucent. Add red wine and cook until liquid is reduced to ¼ c. (50 ml).

3 Add tomatoes and simmer on low heat 3-4 min. Season with salt and pepper.

4 Cook spaghetti in boiling salted water until "al dente". Drain well. Arrange spaghetti and tomato sauce on plates and sprinkle with parsley.

Note:
The original recipe asks for
Parmesan cheese.
The Animal-Friendly Cookbook
recommends using toasted almonds or
fresh parsley instead.

Noodles with Mushrooms

4 - 6 Servings

1 lb. eggless noodles (500 g)

1 lb. fresh Porcini mushrooms (500 g) or 1½ oz. dried Porcini mushrooms (40 g)

2 medium onions, chopped

½c. dry white wine (⅛ l)

3 tbsp. margarine

2 tsp. granulated vegetable bouillon

4 tbsp. chopped parsley

Salt and freshly ground pepper, to taste

Preparation time:

Approx. 45 min.

1 If using dried mushrooms, soak in 3 c. cold water 20 min. Drain and save water. If using fresh mushrooms, clean and finely chop. Sauté onions in half the margarine.

2 Add mushrooms (drained or fresh) and sauté briefly. Add wine and water from soaking dried mushrooms. Cook uncovered until mushrooms are tender and sauce has boiled down.

3 Meanwhile cook noodles in boiling salted water until "al dente". Drain. Season mushroom sauce with vegetable bouillon, salt and pepper.

4 Add remaining margarine. Combine noodles and sauce. Sprinkle with parsley and serve hot.

Tagliatelle alla Salvia

4 - 6 Servings

17 oz. (500 g) eggless tagliatelle noodles

2 tsp. dried sage leaves

5 tbsp. olive oil

Salt

Preparation time:

Approx. 20 min.

1 Cook noodles in salted water until "al dente". Warm oil in a pan, add crushed sage and 2 pinches salt.

2 Add cooked, drained noodles and mix well. Garlic or walnut pieces may be added.

Pasta Vegetable Stir-fry

4 - 6 Servings

14 oz. rigatoni or spaghetti (400 g)

1¾ lbs. vegetables in season (800 g) i.e. carrots, eggplant, zucchini, peppers, cauliflower, broccoli ...

2 medium onions, chopped

2 tbsp. olive oil

2 tsp. granulated vegetable bouillon

Herbs de Provence seasoning, to taste

Salt and freshly ground pepper, to taste

Dash paprika

Preparation time:

Approx. 45 min.

1 Cook pasta in boiling, salted water until "al dente".

2 Meanwhile, cut vegetables into small pieces.

3 Heat oil. Sauté onions, add vegetables and sauté together. Season well, cover and cook on low heat until tender. Add water as needed.

4 Combine with drained pasta and serve at once on preheated plates.

Noodle Salad

4 - 6 Servings

9 oz. spirelli pasta (250 g)

½ each red, green and yellow bell peppers

3½ oz. olives (100 g)

1 carrot

4 tbsp. olive oil

2 tbsp. vinegar

Salt and freshly ground pepper

1 clove garlic

Sprig fresh basil

1 Cook pasta in boiling, salted water until "al dente". Finely chop peppers. Peel carrot, finely chop and blanch. Mince basil.

2 For the dressing, blend well: vinegar, oil, crushed garlic, salt, pepper and basil. Combine dressing, pasta, bell peppers, carrot and olives.

Vegetarian Bolognese Sauce

4 - 6 Servings

1 lb. spaghetti (500 g)

1 onion

2 cloves garlic

1 1/8 c. sunflower seeds
(150 g)

23 oz. pureed tomatoes
(650 g)

1/2 tsp. ground caraway seeds

Salt and freshly ground pepper,
to taste

3 tbsp. olive oil

1 tsp. oregano

5 tbsp. bread crumbs

2 tbsp. olive oil

Preparation time:

Approx. 45 min.

Serving suggestion:
Spaghetti is generally
loved by all guests.
Serve with a fresh Italian
salad and red wine
or fruit juice.

1 Heat 3 tbsp. olive oil in pan. Peel and finely chop onion and garlic. Sauté until translucent.

2 Coarsely chop sunflower seeds in a blender or crush with rolling pin and sauté with onion and garlic.

3 Add pureed tomatoes and mix well.

4 Season with oregano, ground caraway seeds, salt and pepper and simmer on low heat 20 min.

5 Meanwhile, cook spaghetti in boiling salted water until "al dente". Drain well.

6 Toast bread crumbs in 2 tbsp. olive oil until golden brown. Arrange spaghetti on plates, top with Bolognese sauce and sprinkle with bread crumbs.

Vegetable Lasagna

4 - 6 Servings

2 red bell peppers

3 small zuchhini

3 medium onions

1 small carrot

1 package eggless lasagna
noodles

17 oz. tomato sauce (500 ml)
(or 17½ oz. fresh tomatoes)

3½ oz. margarine (100 g)

2 c. oat milk

2 tbsp. cornstarch or
wheat starch

2 tsp. dry white wine

Salt and freshly ground pepper,
to taste

6 tbsp. olive oil

2 cloves garlic

Preparation time:

Approx. 60 min.
Preheat oven 350°F (175°C)

Variation:
With this same recipe
you can prepare many
variations of lasagna
by using seasonal
vegetables, spinach
or mushrooms for the
filling.

1 Peel and finely chop 2½ onions and 1 clove garlic and sauté briefly in 3 tbsp. olive oil. Clean and finely chop bell peppers and zucchini and sauté briefly with the onions and garlic.

2 Tomato sauce: Finely chop second garlic clove and remaining ½ onion. Sauté briefly in oil. Add finely chopped carrot and sauté. Add tomatoes, cook briefly. Season with salt and oregano, and pureé.

3 Béchamel sauce: Melt margarine. Add cornstarch and oat milk, stirring rapidly until smooth. Season with salt, pepper and white wine.

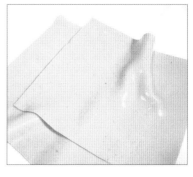

4 Cook lasagna noodles according to package directions.

5 Grease baking dish and layer ingredients: first tomato sauce, then lasagna noodles; then vegetables, and béchamel sauce last.

6 Repeat layers until baking dish is full. Bake 25 min., until golden brown.

Ravioli with Nut Sauce

4 - 6 Servings

1 lb. eggless ravioli (500 g)

2 tbsp. margarine

1 onion

1 clove garlic

3½ oz. chopped nuts – cashews, almonds, hazelnuts (100 g)

3½ oz. water (100 ml)

2 tbsp. margarine

2 tsp. cornstarch

Saffron

Dry white wine

Salt and freshly ground pepper, to taste

Preparation time:

Approx. 45 min.

1 Peel onion and garlic. Chop finely. Heat margarine and sauté onion, garlic and chopped nuts. Set aside.

2 Heat margarine. Add water and cornstarch and mix briskly until smooth. Add white wine, salt and pepper to taste.

3 Combine sauce with onion and nuts, mix well, season to taste and simmer briefly.

4 Cook ravioli in boiling water with salt. Remove carefully from water. Arrange on plates and spoon on the sauce.

Ravioli with Curry

4 - 6 Servings

1 lb. eggless ravioli (500 g)

1 tbsp. margarine

¼ c. coconut milk (50 ml)

¼ c. water (50 ml)

Dry white wine

2 tsp. cornstarch

2 tsp. curry powder

Salt and freshly ground pepper, to taste

1 Heat margarine in pan, add curry powder and sauté. Add coconut milk, water and white wine to taste, stirring briskly. Cook briefly. Season with salt and pepper.

2 Cook ravioli in boiling water according to package directions. Remove carefully from water. Arrange on plates and spoon on the sauce.

Bell Peppers

Whether red, yellow or green, we are a colorful, enjoyable bunch that brightens your plate. Our uniquely hearty flavor emerges when we are eaten raw, as well as fried, steamed, or in salads and many side dishes. We give you a lot of Vitamin C, Vitamin A and other trace elements. Therefore we are — especially if grown in peaceable cultivation — a healthy, refreshing delicacy with a lot of power and life-energy.

»We give you our joy of life!«

Peperonata

4 Servings

2 red bell peppers

2 green bell peppers

4 tomatoes

3 onions

2 clove garlic

4 tbsp. olive oil

Salt and freshly ground pepper, to taste

Pinch of sugar

1 tbsp. fresh thyme leaves

Preparation time:

Approx. 60 min.

Serving suggestion:
Serve with boiled potatoes, rice or polenta.

1 Clean peppers, remove seeds and cut into large diced pieces. Cut tomatoes into large diced pieces.

2 Peel onions and cut into strips. Peel and cut garlic into thin slices.

3 Heat oil in pan and sauté onions until translucent. Add peppers and garlic and sauté 5 min. Add tomatoes.

4 Season with salt, pepper and sugar. Cover and simmer 30 min. on low heat. Sprinkle with thyme leaves and serve.

Stuffed Bell Peppers

4 Servings

4 red bell peppers, with stems

1-2 slices day-old white bread (50 g)

5 tbsp. margarine

1 small onion

1 clove garlic

2 tomatoes

2-3 stalks celery

5½ oz. fresh Shiitake mushrooms (150 g)

2 tbsp. chopped fresh herbs (i.e., parsley, rosemary, marjoram, thyme)

1 c. vegetable broth (250 ml)

Salt and freshly ground pepper, to taste

Preparation time:

Approx. 80 min.
Preheat oven 400°F (200°C)

Serving suggestion:
Serve with rice, boiled or mashed potatoes.

1 Filling: Peel and chop onion and garlic. Wash tomatoes and cube. Clean celery and mushrooms and finely chop.

2 Cut bread into small cubes. Melt 2 tbsp. margarine in a pan, add bread cubes and toast until golden brown.

3 Melt remaining margarine in a pan, add chopped onion and garlic and sauté.

4 Add celery, tomatoes and mushrooms in this order, season with salt and pepper and simmer 5 min. Add chopped herbs and toasted bread cubes.

5 Wash peppers and cut tops off like a lid. Remove seeds, leaving a hollow shell.

6 Fill shells with bread-filling. Lightly coat with oil. Place filled peppers in a baking dish and pour in vegetable broth. Bake 45 min. When half done, cover with aluminum foil to prevent over-browning on top.

Pepper-Potato Goulash

4 Servings

½ lb. red bell peppers (250 g)

½ lb. onions (250 g)

½ lb. carrots (250 g)

½ lb. potatoes (250 g)

1¼ lb. tomatoes (600 g)

5 cloves garlic

4¼ c. water (1 l)

2 heaping tbsp. sweet paprika

1 tsp. sugar

2 tsp. granulated vegetable bouillon

3 oz. oil (100 ml)

Salt and freshly ground pepper, to taste

Hot paprika powder or chili powder to taste

Preparation time:

Approx. 60 min.

Serving suggestion:

Serve with polenta, rice or bread and a red wine.

1 Peel onions, potatoes, and carrots. Wash tomatoes and peppers and cut all in large cubes. Peel garlic and crush.

2 Heat oil in large pan, add onions and garlic and sauté until translucent.

3 Add sweet paprika powder, season with pepper and sauté briefly.

4 Add carrots, tomatoes and peppers. Season with salt and simmer 5 min.

5 Pour in water, bring to a boil, cover and simmer gently 15 min. Season to taste with vegetable bouillon, and hot paprika or chili powder.

6 Add potato pieces and cook 30 min. The longer it simmers, the better it will be. Tastes delicious warmed over.

Parsnips

There was a time in Europe that I was as popular as potatoes are today. Now I have been rediscovered and am glad that you get to know me. Like carrots I am very good raw. I taste somewhat spicy and a little sweet. If I come from the peaceable cultivation of the Farms of New Jerusalem, I contain only what is good.

»I only give you good things!«

Parsnip Fritters

4 Servings

1 lb. parsnips (500 g)

3½ oz. leeks (100 g)

4 tbsp. flour

Water

Salt and freshly ground pepper, to taste

Frying oil

Preparation time:

Approx. 60 min.

Serving suggestion:

Serve with a fresh salad. Also suitable as an appetizer or on a cold buffet.

1 Peel and coarsely grate parsnips. Clean and finely slice leeks.

2 Combine parsnips and leeks with flour and water until it has a consistency that can be formed.

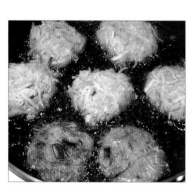

3 Heat oil in pan. Shape small fritters and place in hot oil.

4 Fry on both sides until golden brown. Drain on paper towels and serve at once.

Sautéed Parsnips with Herbs

4 Servings

10½ oz. parsnips (300 g)

1 small carrot

1 small onion

2 tsp. granulated vegetable bouillon

¼ c. water (50 ml)

Pinch of marjoram

¼ c. oil + 1 tbsp. (sunflower or olive)

Salt and freshly ground pepper, to taste

2 tbsp. chopped fresh herbs (parsley, oregano, thyme, etc.)

Preparation time:

Approx. 60 min.

Variation:

Make as curry dish, by using 1 tsp. curry powder in marinade instead of marjoram.

1 Peel and dice parsnips. Peel and thinly slice carrot and onion.

2 Mix well: ¼ c. oil (50 ml), ¼ c. water (50 ml), salt, pepper, vegetable bouillon and marjoram. Add carrot and parsnips and marinade 30 min.

3 Heat 1 tbsp. oil and sauté onion.

4 Add carrot and parsnips and sauté until tender. Sprinkle with fresh herbs and serve.

Glazed Parsnips

4 Servings

7 oz. parsnips (200 g)

4 tbsp. oil

2 tbsp. sugar

½ c. dry white wine or apple juice (100 ml)

Preparation time:

Approx. 20 min.

1 Peel parsnips and cut into thick sticks. Heat oil in pan. Fry parsnips in hot oil.

2 Add sugar and let caramelize. Add white wine and cook until tender.

Rice

$\mathscr{I}$ not only grow in far away Asia but also in Europe, Africa and N. America. I come in many varieties: round-grain rice, long-grain rice, brown or white basmati. Each plant receives its life energy from the water in which it grows and from the earth. And each grain of rice bears within a wonderful force: not only life for a new plant but also for many, many, people! After wheat I am the most important grain worldwide.

Risotto with Mushrooms

4 Servings

1 oz. dried Porcini mushrooms (25 g)

6 oz. fresh Shiitake mushrooms, washed (180 g)

1²/₃ c. round grain rice (300 g)

1 onion

8½ oz. dry white wine (250 ml)

4¼ c. vegetable broth (1 l)

12 oz. water (350 ml)

6 tbsp. margarine

2 tbsp. olive oil

Salt and freshly ground pepper, to taste

2 tbsp. chopped parsley

Preparation time:

Approx. 40 min.

Soak dried Porcini mushrooms approx. 40 min.

1 Soak dried mushrooms in luke-warm water approx. 40 min. Remove, drain and save water.

2 Melt margarine in a pan and sauté finely chopped onion until translucent. Coarsely chop all mushrooms, add to onion and sauté briefly.

3 Add rice and sauté until translucent. Add wine. Mix vegetable broth with saved water and add 1c. to rice. Simmer on medium heat, stirring constantly.

4 Add more broth as absorbed by rice, until creamy but "al dente." Season with salt and pepper. Add parsley.

Vegetarian Paella

4 - 6 Servings

1 large onion

1 clove garlic

2 carrots

1 red bell pepper

1 green bell pepper

1 leek

3½ oz. fresh Shiitake mushrooms (100 g)

4 tbsp. oil

⅔ c. rice (120 g)

½ c dry wine or cider (125 ml)

½ c. water (125 ml)

Salt and freshly ground pepper, to taste

Saffron, to taste (optional)

Garnish:

1 eggplant

1 red bell pepper

Artichoke hearts

Black olives

Lemon slices

Preparation time:

Approx. 45 min.

Serving suggestion:
A typical Spanish dish. Serve paella with fresh salad and a Spanish wine or fruit juice.

1 Peel onion and slice. Clean and slice carrots. Cut cleaned bell peppers in strips. Crush garlic. Clean leek and cut into thin rings.

2 Heat oil in frying pan (paella pan, if possible). Sauté onion and garlic until translucent.

3 Add remaining vegetables and continue to sauté.

4 Add rice and a little saffron. Continue cooking on low heat, stirring well, until rice is translucent.

5 Add wine. Add water and season well. Braise gently on low heat for 15 min. until rice has absorbed liquid.

6 Meanwhile, clean, slice and briefly sauté vegetables for garnish. Garnish paella with vegetables, and finish off with lemon slices.

Beets

»I give you rosy cheeks!«

I am a particularly invaluable gift of nature for you! Do you have an appetite for me? Then you certainly need me. Maybe for iron in your blood? But I am also rich in many other minerals and vitamins. I am pure health, especially when I come from peaceable cultivation, which means I grew in healthy soil.

Red Beets

4 Servings

2 lb. fresh beets (1 kg)

1 red bell pepper

½ c. orange juice (100 ml)

2½ tbsp. margarine

1 tsp. thickener (cornstarch, arrowroot, etc)

Salt and freshly ground pepper, to taste

¹/₃ c. powdered sugar (50 g)

Preparation time:

Approx. 60 min.

Variation:

If red currants are in season, pureé about 1¹/₃ c. (200 g) red currants and add to chopped pepper.

1 Cut roots and leaves from beets, clean well, cover with water and cook about 45 min. until tender.

2 Remove beets from pan, rinse in cold water, drain well, peel and thinly slice. Clean pepper and finely chop.

3 Caramelize powdered sugar in pan over medium heat, stirring constantly. Add orange juice. Add margarine.

4 Mix the thickener with a little water and add. Simmer 5 min. Add chopped pepper and simmer 5 min. Season with salt. Add beet slices and let flavors blend well.

Batter-Coated Beets

4 Servings

1 lb. small beets (500 g)

⅞ c. flour (100 g)

½ c. beer or sparkling mineral water (100 ml)

1½ tbsp. melted margarine

1 small onion

¼ c. dry white wine or apple juice (50 ml)

1¼ c. vegetable broth (300 ml)

1 oz. horseradish, freshly grated or prepared (30 g)

Salt and freshly ground pepper, to taste

¼ tsp. caraway seeds

Frying oil

Garnish with cress sprouts

Preparation time:

Approx. 1½ hours

1 Boil beets whole, unpeeled, with caraway seeds and salt until done. Drain and peel.

2 Batter: Blend flour and beer until smooth. Add melted margarine and salt. Let stand 30 min.

3 Sauce: Cook finely chopped onion in white wine. Add vegetable stock and boil down to approx. ½ c. (100 ml). Add horseradish, salt and pepper and pureé with a mixer.

4 Using a fork, dip whole beets into the batter, then deep fry in ¼ in. hot oil until golden brown. Remove with a slotted spoon and drain well. Arrange with the sauce on plates. Garnish with cress sprouts.

Beets Carpaccio

4 Servings

1 lb. beets (500 g)

1 onion

1 carrot

2 dill pickles

Salt to taste

3 tbsp. olive oil

1 tbsp. vinegar (e.g. raspberry vinegar)

1 tsp. mustard

Preparation time:

Approx. 70 min.

1 Cook beets in boiling water approx. 60 min. Peel and thinly slice. Dice carrot and blanch in boiling water 2 min. Chop pickles and onion.

2 For the dressing, blend vinegar, mustard, salt and olive oil. Combine beet slices with dressing and arrange attractively with diced carrot, pickles and onion.

Brussels Sprouts

»A rosy greeting from nature for you«

Although my rose-like sprouts are fine and delicate, I am really a cabbage and very healthy, because of my vitamins, minerals and much more. Whether boiled, steamed or braised, I simply taste delicious. And if I come from peaceable cultivation, I certainly have absorbed no poisons and give you only what is good!

Brussels Sprouts Nut Crumble

4 Servings

2 lb. Brussels sprouts
(ca. 750 g)

3 tbsp. margarine

2 oz. ground hazelnuts (50 g)

½ c. bread crumbs (50 g)

Salt and freshly ground pepper,
to taste

Dash caraway seeds, ground

Preparation time:

Approx. 40 min.

Serving suggestion:
Serve with rice or parsley-potatoes and a fresh winter salad.

1 Remove outer leaves and stems from Brussels sprouts and wash.

2 Cook Brussels sprouts in boiling salted water 5-10 min. until almost done. Drain well.

3 Melt margarine in frying pan. Add ground nuts and bread crumbs and sauté to a golden brown, stirring constantly.

4 Cut Brussels sprouts in half and quarter pieces, add to crumb mixture and fry briefly. Flavor with salt, pepper and caraway seeds.

Brussels Sprouts Au Gratin

4 Servings

18 oz. Brussels sprouts (500 g)

1 onion

2 tbsp. margarine

2 tbsp. dry white wine

½ c. pine nuts (75 g)

2 tbsp. flour

1 c. oat milk (250 ml)

Dash nutmeg

Salt and freshly ground pepper, to taste

Preparation time:

Approx. 60 min.
Preheat oven 400°F (200°C)

Serving suggestion:
Serve with rice,
boiled potatoes or simply
with bread.

1 Clean Brussels sprouts, cook in boiling salted water 8-10 min. until "al dente". Drain and rinse with cold water.

2 Heat pan. Peel, dice and sauté onion in 1 tbsp. margarine. Add ¼ c. (40 g) pine nuts to onions.

3 Béchamel sauce: Melt remaining margarine, add flour and brown lightly. Add wine and oat milk and stir until smooth. Season with salt, pepper and nutmeg and simmer 10 min.

4 Place Brussels sprouts in an ovenproof dish and season with pepper and nutmeg. Pour béchamel sauce over sprouts. Sprinkle onion mixture and remaining pine nuts on top. Bake 15 min.

Brussels Sprouts Salad

4 Servings

18 oz. Brussels sprouts (500 g)

1 onion

2 tbsp. parsley

Salt to taste

2 tbsp. olive oil

1 tbsp. vinegar

Preparation time:

Approx. 30 min.

1 Clean Brussels sprouts and remove any yellow leaves. Cook in boiling salted water 10 min. until done. Drain and rinse with cold water.

2 Slice Brussels sprouts. Finely chop onion and parsley and combine with Brussels sprouts. Flavor with salt, oil and vinegar.

Salad Greens

In our family we have many, many varieties – one fresher and crunchier than the other. And the possibilities for our use are just as manifold: raw, enhanced with fruits or wild herbs, braised or au gratin. With imagination you can create many tasty dishes with us. Whether in winter or summer, we offer you a fresh side dish containing many vitamins, minerals, folic acid and essential bitter essence.

»We give you many good things for your body!«

Arugula with Shiitake Mushrooms

4 Servings

5¼ oz. fresh Shiitake mushrooms (150 g)

3 tomatoes

3½ oz. arugula (100 g)

4 tbsp. croutons

1 tbsp. margarine

Salt, freshly ground pepper, to taste

2 tbsp. olive oil

1 tbsp. balsamic vinegar

Preparation time:

Approx. 25 min.

1 Gently clean mushrooms and coarsely chop. Sauté mushrooms in hot margarine.

2 Rinse arugula well. Wash and quarter tomatoes.

3 Prepare croutons (page 42). In a small bowl, blend well vinegar, oil, salt and pepper.

4 Attractively arrange arugula, tomatoes and sautéed mushrooms on a serving plate. Sprinkle with dressing and top with croutons.

Braised Belgian Endive

4 - 6 Servings

4 Belgian endives

1 onion, chopped

1 tbsp. sugar

Juice of 1 lemon

1/3 c. dry white wine (80 ml)

¾ c. chopped parsley (50 g)

2 tbsp. toasted slivered almonds

Salt and freshly ground pepper, to taste

1 tbsp. sunflower oil

2 tbsp. margarine

Preparation time:

Approx. 45 min.

Serving suggestion:

Serve with rice or mashed potatoes. Apple juice may be used instead of white wine.

1 Clean endives and cook in boiling salted water with a dash of lemon juice for 5 min. Remove from pan and drain.

2 Peel, chop and sauté onion in some oil in a large pan.

3 Add endives and sear. Add 1 tbsp. sugar and let brown.

4 Add white wine, and season well with salt and pepper. Arrange on plates and sprinkle with parsley and toasted almond slices.

Lamb's Lettuce with Belgian Endive

4 Servings

3½ oz. lamb's lettuce (maché) (100 g)

2 Belgian endives

2 apples

2 tbsp. apple cider vinegar

3 tbsp. sunflower oil

2 handfuls croutons

Salt and freshly ground pepper, to taste

1 Rinse lamb's lettuce 2 to 3 times with plenty of water. Drain well. Wash endives and separate into single leaves. Slice apples.

2 Attractively arrange lamb's lettuce, endive leaves and apple slices on a serving plate. For the dressing: Blend oil, vinegar, salt and pepper together. Sprinkle over salad and top with croutons.

Fennel-Orange Salad

4 Servings

4 oranges

1 onion

1 1/3 lb. fennel (600 g)

3 oz. black olives (80 g)

2 tbsp. lemon juice

5 tbsp. orange juice

1 tsp. paprika

3 tbsp. olive oil

2 tbsp. chopped parsley

Salt and freshly ground pepper, to taste

Preparation time:

Approx. 20 min.

1 Peel oranges, remove white membrane and separate into segments. Peel onion and slice into thin rings.

2 Wash fennel, remove roots and green stems. Cut in thin lengthwise slices (2 mm).

3 Dressing: Combine lemon juice, orange juice, paprika, salt and pepper Stir well. Add parsley. Add oil last.

4 Arrange fennel, onion rings and orange segments on plates. Place black olives on top and sprinkle with dressing and chopped parsley.

Endive Salad

4 Servings

1 endive

2 oz. winter purslane or cress (50 g)

1 onion, 1 red bell pepper

2 tbsp. chives, chopped

1 tbsp. mustard

6 tbsp. oil

2 tbsp. each vinegar and water

3/4 c. chopped walnuts (100 g)

Salt and freshly ground pepper, to taste

1 Wash endive and purslane well. Cut endive into small pieces. Peel and slice onion into thin rings. Clean red pepper and finely chop.

2 Dressing: Mix well oil, mustard, water, chopped walnuts, vinegar, salt and pepper. Sprinkle salad with dressing and then with chives.

Lentil Salad

4 Servings

1¼ c. small brown lentils (250g)

1 large onion

3 oz. leeks (80 g)

2 carrots

2 tomatoes

1 or 2 bay leaves

4 cloves

4 tbsp. olive oil

2 tbsp. chopped parsley

1 tbsp. mustard

Pinch of sugar

6 tbsp. vinegar

Salt and freshly ground pepper, to taste

Preparation time:

Approx. 50 min.
Soak lentils overnight

1 Rinse lentils and soak overnight. Drain and cook with bay leaves, cloves and 1 tbsp. vinegar in approx. 3¼ c. (750 ml) salted water 35 min.

2 Dressing: Blend remaining vinegar, mustard, sugar, oil, salt and pepper.

3 Peel carrots, cut in small cubes and blanch in hot water 5 min. Clean leeks, cut into thin strips and blanch 3 min.

4 Peel onion and finely chop. Dice tomatoes. Combine vegetables with lentils, dressing and parsley.

Radicchio Salad with Walnuts

4 Servings

9 oz. radicchio (250 g)

1 small apple

4 dates

1 oz. walnuts (30 g)

1 tbsp. mustard

6 tbsp. oil

2 tbsp. water

2 tbsp. vinegar or lemon juice

Salt and freshly ground pepper, to taste

1 Clean and cut radicchio. Toast walnuts in a dry pan. Remove seeds from dates and cut into small pieces. Arrange salad on plates and add nuts and dates.

2 Dressing: Chop very finely 10 g walnuts and blend with mustard, oil, water, vinegar or lemon juice, salt and pepper. Pour dressing over salad. Garnish with apple slices.

Vinaigrette Salad Dressing

4 Servings

1 large tomato

2 cloves garlic

1½ oz. leeks (40 g)

Juice of ½ lemon

⅓ c. olive oil (80 ml)

2 tbsp. chopped parsley

2 tbsp. mustard

Salt and freshly ground pepper,
to taste

1 Wash and dice tomato. Peel garlic and mince. Clean leeks and slice into thin rings.

2 Blend lemon juice, olive oil and mustard. Add tomato, garlic, leeks, parsley, salt and pepper, mixing well. Goes well with grilled or fried vegetables.

Avocado Salad Dressing

4 Servings

1 avocado

Juice of 1 lemon

Salt and freshly ground pepper,
to taste

Serving suggestion:
Serve with green salad, tomato salad, fried vegetables or on bread.

1 Peel, half, remove seed and dice avocado.

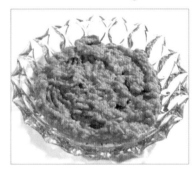

2 Pureé with lemon juice, salt and pepper.

Orange Salad Dressing

4 Servings

2 oranges

Pinch of sugar

6 tbsp. oil

1 tbsp. chives

Salt and freshly ground pepper,
to taste

1 Squeeze juice from oranges. Finely chop chives.

2 Mix all ingredients together. Tasty on green salad, and good with apples.

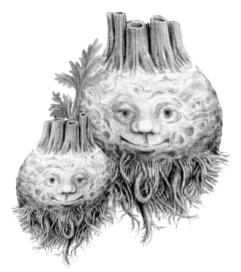

»We are alive!«

Celeriac

I am a magnificent, nourishing root and available all winter long. Some people like me because I am deliciously crunchy and have a spicy taste. Others like me because of my cleansing effect or my high mineral content. You can use me in many ways: as a vegetable, in soups, as a breaded schnitzel, or as a delicious salad ...

Celeriac Schnitzel

4 Servings

14 oz. celeriac (400 g)

½ c. all-purpose flour (60 g)

½ c. water (100 ml)

1 c. fine bread crumbs (100 g)

6 tbsp. oil

Salt to taste

Juice of one lemon

Freshly ground pepper to taste

2 tsp. granulated vegetable bouillon

Sesame seeds

Preparation time:

Approx. 40 min.

Serving suggestion:

Serve with your favorite tomato or herb sauce, with potato salad and steamed vegetables.

1 Peel celeriac and slice ½ in. thick (1 cm). Cook slices in boiling salted water with lemon juice 8 min.

2 Coating: Whisk flour and water until smooth. Season with salt, pepper and granulated vegetable bouillon.

3 Remove celeriac slices from water, drain well. Dip slices in coating, then breadcrumbs and lastly in sesame seeds.

4 Heat oil in a pan and fry breaded celeriac slices until golden brown. Drain on paper towel. Serve warm.

Celeriac with Caper Sauce

4 Servings

14 oz. celeriac (400 g)

1 onion

2 tbsp. capers for sauce

1 tbsp. capers for garnish

2 tbsp. mustard

4 tbsp. oil

4 tbsp. water

2 tsp. granulated vegetable bouillon

Salt and freshly ground pepper, to taste

Preparation time:

Approx. 1½ hours

Serving suggestion:

As an appetizer or in a cold buffet

1 Clean and peel the celeriac, cut in ½ in. thick (1 cm) slices.

2 Cook slices in boiling salted water approx. 10 min.

3 Sauce: Blend chopped onion, 2 tbsp. capers, mustard, oil and water with mixer. Season with salt, pepper and granulated vegetable bouillon.

4 Drain celeriac slices, add to sauce and marinate approx. 1 hour. Arrange on serving plate and garnish with remaining capers.

Celeriac Salad

4 Servings

1½ lb. celeriac (700 g)

1 orange

7 oz. coconut milk (200 ml)

¼ c. walnuts, halves or broken (20 g)

Salt and freshly ground pepper, to taste

2 tbsp. vinegar

Preparation time:

Approx. 30 min.

1 Clean, peel and coarsely grate celeriac. Cut orange into small pieces. For dressing: Blend coconut milk well with vinegar, salt and pepper.

2 Combine celeriac, orange pieces and walnuts with the dressing. Arrange in a salad bowl and garnish with additional orange slices and walnuts.

154

Spinach

»We are tender and give you a lot of minerals.«

$\mathscr{A}$lmost everyone knows me from childhood on. My leaves are tender and healthy for your body. I am mostly cooked and used in a variety of dishes, such as noodles, in casseroles, soups or mixed with other vegetables. My leaves are also delicious raw, as a salad or on bread and give you many, many minerals. I am especially healthy when I am allowed to grow on healthy soil from peaceable cultivation.

Spinach Spätzle

4 Servings

$3^1/_3$ c. flour (400 g)

7 oz. cooked spinach (200 g)

$^2/_3$ c. water (150 ml)

1-2 onions

7 tbsp. margarine (100 g)

1 tsp. salt

Preparation time:

Approx. 40 min.

Serving suggestion:
Serve with a mushroom sauce and steamed vegetables.
Instead of spinach, add 3 tsp. of various chopped herbs to the dough.

1 Finely chop cooked spinach. In a bowl blend spinach well with flour. Gradually add water while beating constantly, until bubbles appear.

2 Peel and thinly slice onions. Melt margarine in pan, add onions and sauté until golden brown. Set aside.

3 Press spinach-batter by portions through a spätzle maker or through the holes of a colander into boiling salted water. Spätzle is done when it floats to the surface.

4 Remove spätzle from water with a slotted spoon and combine in pan with the onions. Arrange attractively on a serving plate.

Spinach Dumplings

4 Servings

1 lb. spinach (500 g)

½ lb. white day-old bread,
approx. 6-7 slices (250 g)

½ c. oat milk (100 ml)

²/₃ c. flour (80 g)

4 tbsp. margarine

1 clove garlic

8 sage leaves

Dash nutmeg

Salt and freshly ground pepper,
to taste

Preparation time:

Approx. 40 min.

Serving suggestion:
Serve with arugula salad
and an Italian white wine.

1 Cube bread, mix with oat milk and let soak.

2 Clean spinach and cook briefly in boiling salted water. Remove from water, press out moisture and finely chop. Add to soaked bread.

3 Add flour, season well with salt, pepper and nutmeg. Blend well.

4 Using a soup spoon, shape dumplings from this dough.

5 Place dumplings in boiling salted water and simmer on low heat 5-7 min. Remove dumplings and drain well.

6 Melt margarine in a frying pan. Stir sage leaves in the margarine. Add dumplings and sauté briefly.

Tomatoes

»We share our joy with you!«

*W*ith our happy color, our wonderful aroma and our refreshing flavor, we are a favorite vegetable all over the world. Prepared raw as a salad, we delight you with our freshness. And we pass on to you the vigor of the sun, which allows us to grow and ripen. As a sauce, stuffed, or au gratin, we enrich any dish. Our full aroma develops best when we are allowed to grow in peaceable cultivation, without solid or liquid manure, without chemicals or sewage sludge.

Tomato Soup

4 Servings

1 lb. tomatoes (500 g)

1 small carrot

1 large onion

1 clove garlic

2 tbsp. olive oil

$2^{1}/_{8}$ c. water (500 ml)

Salt and freshly ground pepper, to taste

Fresh basil

1 tsp. oregano

Preparation time:

Approx. 45 min.

Serving suggestion:
This soup tastes delicious with lots of fresh basil.

1 Peel and finely chop garlic and onion. Peel and slice carrot. Clean and quarter tomatoes.

2 Heat oil in pan. Add onion and garlic and sauté until translucent. Add carrot and let simmer 5 min.

3 Season with salt, pepper and oregano. Add tomatoes and water and simmer 30 min.

4 Blend with a mixer and garnish with fresh basil.

Tomatoes Stuffed with Rice

4 - 6 Servings

12 ripe, but firm tomatoes

3 tbsp. long grain rice

4 tbsp. chopped parsley

4 tbsp. olive oil

Dash nutmeg

Salt and freshly ground pepper,
to taste

Preparation time:

Approx. 60 min
Preheat oven 340°F (170°C)

Serving Suggestion:
Serve with a fresh
Italian salad.

1 Boil rice until barely done. Drain well and set aside.

2 Wash tomatoes and cut top off in the form of a lid. Scoop out inside flesh from tomatoes.

3 Chop tomato tops and scooped-out flesh and mix with rice, parsley and 2 tbsp. oil. Season with salt, pepper and nutmeg.

4 Place tomatoes in greased ovenproof dish. Fill tomatoes with rice mixture and sprinkle with remaining oil. Bake 30 min.

Tomatoes Provençale

4 Servings

4 large tomatoes

4 tbsp. bread crumbs

4 cloves garlic

2 tbsp. olive oil

Salt to taste

Herbs de Provence, to taste

Preparation time:

Approx. 20 Min.
Preheat oven 425°F (220°C)

1 Cut tomatoes in half and salt. Peel and press garlic. Combine bread crumbs, garlic and herbs and blend well.

2 Cover tomato halves with breadcrumb mixture and sprinkle with oil. Place on greased baking sheet and bake 10 min.

Gazpacho

4 Servings

3-4 slices white bread without crust

2 small onions

3 cloves garlic

2-3 red bell peppers

4 tomatoes

1-2 cucumbers

3 tbsp. olive oil

2 c. cold vegetable stock (500 ml)

Salt and freshly ground pepper, to taste

12 pitted green olives

Fresh herbs (e.g., oregano, basil)

Preparation time:

Approx. 1½ hours

Serving suggestion: A favorite, refreshing soup for summer.

1 Cube bread. Soak ⅓ bread cubes briefly in water. Then squeeze out water. Combine soaked cubes with one chopped onion and two chopped garlic cloves, add 2 tbsp. oil and pureé.

2 Clean and finely chop red peppers and tomatoes. Peel and finely chop cucumbers.

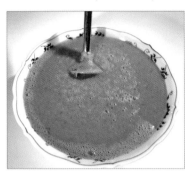

3 Combine vegetables with pureed bread mixture and blend well with electric mixer. Season to taste and refrigerate for 1 hour. Stir in the cold vegetable stock.

4 Toast remaining bread cubes with one chopped clove garlic and 1 tbsp. oil until golden brown. Cut olives in half. Serve soup in bowls and garnish with toasted croutons and olive halves.

Tomato Cocktail

Yield: Two cups

2 medium ripe tomatoes

10 oz. water (300 ml)

Pinch of pepper

3 pinches salt

Preparation time:

Approx. 15 min.

1 Cut tomatoes and mix well with water, salt and pepper.

2 Pureé with an electric mixer. Pour into two glasses and serve chilled.

Zucchini

We are a sunny vegetable from southern climes and belong to the squash family. Our tender pulp and mild flavor make us suitable for many delicious dishes. You can serve us with noodles or rice, or make hearty au gratins, and side dishes from us. We also like to mix with other summer vegetables and taste best with many fresh herbs.

»We give you the strength of the sun that is in us!«

Stuffed Zucchini

4 Servings

4 large or 8 small zucchini

$^2/_3$ c. cooked rice (100 g)

1 lb. tomatoes (500 g)

1 chopped onion

1-2 cloves minced garlic

2 tbsp. olive oil

1½ tbsp. margarine

½ c. hot vegetable broth (125 ml)

Salt and freshly ground pepper, to taste

2 tsp. paprika

Pinch of sugar

2 tbsp. parsley

2 tsp. each dill, oregano

Preparation time:

Approx. 60 min.
Preheat oven 400°F (200°C)

1 Clean zucchini and cut in half lengthwise. Scoop out pulp and cut into small cubes. Dice 2 tomatoes and cut another 2 tomatoes in thin slices.

2 Combine zucchini pulp, rice, diced tomatoes and $^1/_3$ of chopped onion. Mix well and flavor with salt, pepper and herbs.

3 Tomato sauce: Chop remaining tomatoes. Sauté remaining onion and minced garlic in olive oil until translucent. Add chopped tomatoes and spices. Simmer 15 min. Flavor with oregano.

4 Fill zucchini halves with rice mixture and place in an oven-proof dish. Place tomato slices on top. Pour vegetable stock into dish around zucchini. Bake 25 min. Serve with tomato sauce.

Zucchini Gratin

4 Servings

7 small zucchini

1 onion

½ c. well-seasoned vegetable stock (125 ml)

3½ oz. black olives (100 g)

2 tbsp. olive oil

2 cloves garlic

5 tbsp. chopped parsley

Salt and freshly ground pepper, to taste

1/3 c. bread crumbs (30 g)

Preparation time:

Approx. 45 min.

Preheat oven 400°F (200°C)

Serving suggestion:
Serve with parsley-potatoes, rice or bread and salad.

1 Remove stems from zucchini and quarter lengthwise. Cut into ¾ in. (2 cm) pieces. Peel and mince garlic.

2 Rinse parsley, finely chop and combine with garlic and olives. Peel, chop and sauté onions in olive oil until translucent.

3 Add zucchini pieces to onions and steam on low heat 10 min. Season with salt and pepper. Add parsley and olives.

4 Put everything in a greased casserole dish and add vegetable stock. Sprinkle with bread crumbs. Bake in oven until golden brown, about 15 min.

Zucchini Provençale

4 Servings

2 lb. zucchini (1 kg)

Salt and freshly ground pepper, to taste

4 tbsp. olive oil

Herbs de Provence

Preparation time:

Approx. 1½ hours

1 Slice zucchini at an angle and coat with a marinade of 2 tbsp. oil, pepper, salt and Herbs de Provence. Let stand 1 hour.

2 Heat 2 tbsp. oil in pan and fry marinated zucchini slices. Serve as an appetizer or main dish with white bread.

Onions

Since the time of pharaohs, I have been valued and found indispensable as a vegetable or seasoning. My flavor is incomparably zesty and rounds off any dish, raw in salads or on bread, cooked in sauces, stews, soups and much more. I give your body many vitamins and minerals such as potassium and folic acid. So, I am good for you in every respect and wish you a lot of strength from peaceable nature.

Onion Bruschetta

4 - 6 Servings

12 slices white bread

2 lb. onions (1 kg)

3 tbsp. small black olives

Basil leaves

4 tbsp. olive oil

Salt and freshly ground pepper, to taste

2 tbsp. thyme

Preparation time:

Approx. 35 min.
Preheat oven 400°F (200°C)

Variation:
While sautéing onions, add paprika or curry, to taste.

1 Toast bread slices in oven or in a toaster until light brown.

2 Peel onions and cut into thin strips.

3 Heat oil in pan, add onions and sauté until translucent. Season with salt, pepper and thyme.

4 Combine warm onions with olives and basil leaves and serve on toast.

170

Onion Soup

4 - 6 Servings

3-4 large onions

1 tbsp. flour

7 oz. dry white wine (200 ml)

3 c. vegetable stock (700 ml)

6 tbsp. margarine (75 g)

Salt and freshly ground pepper, to taste

Preparation time:

Approx. 40 min.

1 Peel onions and cut into thin rings.

2 Melt margarine in pan, add onions and sauté on low heat 20 min.

3 Add flour. Add wine and vegetable stock, stirring constantly.

4 Season with salt and pepper. Serve hot with toasted bread or croutons.

Onion Rings

4 Servings

2 large onions

1 c. flour (100 g)

3½ oz. beer or carbonated water (100 ml)

1½ tbsp. melted margarine

Salt to taste

Oil for deep frying

1 Peel onions and cut into thin rings. For batter: Blend flour and beer with wire whisk until smooth. Blend in melted margarine.

2 Heat ¼ in. oil in a pan. Using a fork, dip onion rings one at a time into batter and deep fry until golden brown. Good as an appetizer

Onion Relish

4 - 6 Servings

3 medium onions

½c dry white wine or apple juice (125 ml)

1 tbsp. vinegar

1 tsp. paprika

2 tbsp. oil

Salt and freshly ground pepper, to taste

Preparation time:

Approx. 40 min.

Variation:
Instead of paprika, season with curry powder, ginger and some sugar.

1 Peel onions and cut into large pieces or slices.

2 Heat oil in frying pan. Add onions and sauté.

3 Add wine and vinegar. Season well with salt, pepper and paprika.

4 Simmer until liquid has cooked into the onions.

Glazed Onions

4 Servings

10 very small onions

4 tbsp. oil

2 tbsp. sugar

3½ oz dry white wine or apple juice (100 ml)

Salt to taste

Preparation time:

Approx. 40 min.

1 Peel small onions. Heat oil in frying pan, add onions and sear. Add sugar and let brown.

2 Add wine and salt. Simmer 30 min. Serve cold as an appetizer or with an aperitif.

Mixed Vegetables

»We are happy to serve you!«

𝒲e are children from God's garden and are happy to serve you. We delight you with our variety, with our colors and shapes and are full of vitality for you! We give thanks to the Creator for the strength of the Sun and the Earth, for the rain and the warmth that lets us grow and flourish in good soil and through peaceable cultivation. It is this strength and happiness that we pass on to you.

Vegetable Soup

4 Servings

3½ oz. white beans (100 g)

½ leek

1 carrot

½ celeriac

1 large potato

1-2 zucchini

½ c. cauliflower

2 tbsp. olive oil

8½ c. vegetable stock (2 l)

Salt and freshly ground pepper, to taste

5 tbsp. chopped parsley

Preparation time:

Approx. 60 min.
Soak beans overnight.

Serving suggestion:

Add rice or small noodles.

1 Soak beans overnight in cold water. Next day, boil approx. 30 min., without salt!

2 Clean and cut all vegetables into bite-size pieces. Wash and chop parsley.

3 Heat oil in pan and sauté leek, carrot and celeriac. Add potato, zucchini and cauliflower.

4 Add beans and vegetable stock and let simmer approx. 30 min. Season with salt and pepper. Sprinkle with parsley and serve with white bread.

Asian Vegetable Bowl

4 Servings

2 large potatoes

1 red bell pepper

4 onions

2-3 small carrots

5 oz. fresh green beans (150 g)

10 oz. coconut milk (300 ml)

1 tbsp. curry powder

3 tbsp. vegetable oil

½ c. water (ca. 100 ml)

Salt and freshly ground pepper, to taste

½ tsp. ground coriander

Preparation time:

Approx. 50 min.

Serving suggestion:

Good with rice, or simply white bread and black or jasmine tea.

1 Peel and dice potatoes. Clean and dice pepper into large pieces. Peel onions and carrots and cut into small sticks. Cut green beans into 1 in. pieces (3 cm).

2 Heat oil in a large frying pan. Add onions, potatoes and carrots and fry at high heat 3 min.

3 Add remaining vegetables and fry 5 min.

4 Add curry powder, blend well and continue to fry briefly.

5 Add coconut milk and water. Season with salt, pepper and coriander.

6 Cover and let simmer on low heat until potatoes and carrots are tender. Add water as necessary.

Greek Vegetable Stew

4 - 6 Servings

1 lb. eggplant (500 g)

2 onions

1 green bell pepper

1 yellow bell pepper

2-3 small zucchini

9 oz. fresh green beans
(250 g)

1 lb. tomatoes (500 g)

4 cloves garlic

6 tbsp. olive oil

1 tsp. sugar

2 bay leaves

2 tsp. oregano

1 tsp. thyme

Several sprigs parsley, chopped

Salt and freshly ground pepper,
to taste

½ tsp. ground coriander

Preparation time:

Approx. 60 min.

Serving suggestion:
Serve with rice
or bread.

1 Wash eggplant and cut into ¾ in. (2 cm) cubes. Sprinkle with salt and let stand to lose bitter taste. Dry with paper towel.

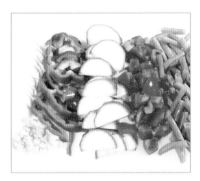

2 Peel and slice onions. Clean peppers, core and cut into rings. Wash and slice zucchini. Clean green beans and cut into pieces. Mince garlic and cube tomatoes.

3 Heat olive oil in large frying pan. Sauté onions. Sprinkle with sugar and let caramelize slightly.

4 Add eggplant and brown.

5 Add garlic and remaining vegetables (except tomatoes) and brown, stirring constantly 5 min.

6 Add tomatoes, season with salt, pepper and herbs (except parsley). Cover and let simmer on low heat 15 min. Sprinkle with parsley just before serving.

Vegetable-Filled Pancakes

4 - 6 Servings

1²/₃ c. cornmeal (250 g)

2 c. flour (250g)

4¼ c. water (1 l)

2 medium onions

8¾ oz. seasonal vegetables –
carrots, zucchini, swiss chard,
etc. (250 g)

Salt and freshly ground pepper,
to taste

Oil

Preparation time:

Approx. 40 min.

Variation:

Pancakes are also tasty
filled with fresh herbs,
thinly sliced fresh tomato,
cucumber or lettuce leaf.

1 Mix cornmeal, flour, salt and water until smooth and thick, a fluid batter. Let stand 30 min.

2 Meanwhile, peel onions, cut into thin slices and sauté in oil. Clean vegetables, cut into pieces or strips and sauté with onion. Season with salt and pepper.

3 Heat oil in frying pan. Ladle small amount batter into pan and cook to a golden brown.

4 Turn pancake and brown the other side. Fill with vegetables.

Frittata

4 - 6 Servings

1²/₃ c. cornmeal (250 g)

2 c. flour (250g)

4¼ c. water (1 liter)

2 medium onions

8¾ oz. (250 g) seasonal
vegetables – carrots, zucchini,
swiss chard, etc.

Salt, pepper, freshly ground

Oil

1 Mix batter as in recipe above. Peel onions and sauté in oil. Clean vegetables and thinly cut. Sauté briefly with onions.

2 Ladle batter into pan with sautéed vegetables. Brown on both sides.

Veggie Party

10½ oz. cocktail or small tomatoes (300 g)

2 small cucumbers

1 red bell pepper

3 celery stalks

¾ c. vegan herb spread

¾ c. spicy hot vegan spread

3 tsp. vegan mayonnaise

3 tbsp. finely chopped, fresh, mixed herbs (basil, parsley, dill)

Salt, to taste

Basil and parsley for garnish

Preparation time:

Approx. 40 min.

Serving suggestion:
For a cold buffet, garnish platter with filled vegetables and Bruschetta.

1 Clean tomatoes and cut in half. Clean red pepper, cut lengthwise 1 in. wide, then halve. Cut cucumbers in half, lengthwise. Clean celery, cut 1½ in. lengths.

2 Hollow out and salt tomato and cucumber halves. Mix herb spread well with mayonnaise and finely chopped herbs.

3 Put mixture in a pastry decorator tube and fill the hollowed tomato and cucumber halves. Garnish with basil and parsley.

4 Put spicy spread in decorator tube and fill celery and red pepper pieces. Arrange filled veggies attractively on serving platter.

Bruschetta

4 Servings

Half a baguette

2 medium tomatoes

Olive oil

4 tsp. pesto, or wild garlic sauce

A few black olives

Fresh basil

1 Slice baguette. Toast baguette slices in pan of hot oil until golden brown on both sides. Clean tomatoes and dice small.

2 Spread toasted slices with pesto. Lay tomato pieces on top and garnish with olive and basil leaf.

Fruits & Deserts

»We are refreshing and give you pleasure!«

Our variety is remarkable and each one of us has our own special nature. Some are hearty, some mild, some are sour, some sweet, some are crunchy, but always, we have our own unique flavor. And in just as many ways, we can please you as appetizers, main dishes, deserts, salads, snacks, in cakes and much more. We are refreshing and give you pleasure with our colors and flavors. Fruit is healthy, especially when we are able to grow and ripen naturally, without chemicals.

Banana Flambé

4 Servings

6 bananas

6 tbsp. margarine

6 tbsp. sugar

3 tbsp. Grand Marnier

3 tbsp. rum

Preparation time:

Approx. 25 min.

Variation:

You can also try this recipe with pineapple chunks. A cool lemon sherbet also goes well with flambéed fruit.

1 Peel bananas, cut in half lengthwise and then cut each length in half.

2 Melt margarine in a frying pan. Add sugar and brown while stirring. Add bananas.

3 On high heat, brown banana pieces on both sides. Add Grand Marnier and rum.

4 Tip the pan slightly and carefully set alcohol on fire. Arrange flambéed bananas on plates.

Pears in Red Wine

4 Servings

1½ l red wine (e.g., Spanish Rioja)

1⅓ c. sugar (280 g)

8 pears

Stick of cinnamon

2 cloves

2 lemon slices

2 allspice seeds, whole, untreated

Salt and freshly ground pepper, to taste

Preparation time:

Approx. 1½ hours

Serving suggestion:

As a warm desert with cinnamon ice cream.

1 Combine wine, sugar and lemon slices in a large pan and bring to boil. Let cook and reduce liquid by half.

2 Peel pears, but leave stems on. Remove blossom ends.

3 Place pears in red wine syrup. Add spices. Bring to a boil and let simmer 15 min.

4 Remove pears with a slotted spoon and place on serving plate. Further reduce syrup, pour over pears, and serve with cookies.

Chocolate Crème

4 Servings

3½ oz. cooking chocolate (100 g)

2 tbsp. water

17 oz. coconut milk (500 ml)

2 tbsp. cornstarch (or other thickener)

Sugar as desired

4 tbsp. margarine

Preparation time:

Approx. 30 min.

1 Melt chocolate in a pan with 2 tbsp. water and 2 tbsp. coconut milk.

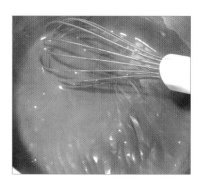

2 Stir cornstarch into remaining coconut milk. Blend into melted chocolate. Bring to a boil stirring constantly. Add margarine. Fill dessert bowls and refrigerate.

Rice Pudding with Orange Salad

4 Servings

4¼ c. rice milk (1 l)

³/₈ c. short grain rice (80 g)

4 tbsp. cornstarch, or other thickener

½ c. sugar (100 g)

1 ¹/₈ c. slivered almonds (100 g)

1 tsp. vanilla flavor or
1 vanilla bean, split

1 orange

¹/₃ c. pine nuts (50 g)

Small tea cookies for decoration

Orange salad:

4 oranges

8 dried dates

¹/₃ c. raisins (50 g)

½ tsp. ground cinnamon

Juice of 1 orange

Preparation time:

Approx. 40 min.

Serving suggestion:
Serve as desert with fresh fruit juice.

1 Soak raisins in orange juice 30 min. Toast pine nuts in dry frying pan. Peel 1 orange and cut into thin slices.

2 Rice pudding: In a pan, bring rice milk to a boil. Gradually add rice, while stirring. Reduce heat and simmer 20 min.

3 Dissolve cornstarch in a little water and stir into rice. Stir in sugar, almonds and vanilla bean (if using vanilla flavor, wait to add after cooking). Cook pudding until thick.

4 If using vanilla bean, remove. Place in dessert bowls, garnish with orange slices, raisins, half the pine nuts and small cookies. Sprinkle with cinnamon.

5 Orange salad: Peel 4 oranges, removing as much white membrane as possible, and cut into thin slices of approx. ¼ in. (4 mm).

6 Pit dates and cut into small pieces. Arrange orange slices on plates and sprinkle with cut dates and remaining pine nuts.

"Poor Knights" with Cherry-Red Wine Syrup

4 Servings

5 oz. rice milk (150 ml)

2 tbsp. sugar

1 tbsp. cinnamon

Half a baguette

Margarine

Batter:

3½ oz. water (100 ml)

3½ oz. cider or apple juice (100 ml)

²/3 c. flour (75 g)

Red wine syrup:

3 tbsp. sugar

2 tbsp. margarine

7 oz. cherries, fresh, frozen, or canned (200 g)

3½ oz. dry red wine (100 ml)

Preparation time:

Approx. 40 min.

Variation:

Instead of red wine, use sour cherry juice.

1 Cut baguette into 8 slices approx. ¾ in. thick (2 cm).

2 Mix rice milk with sugar and cinnamon. For batter: Blend flour, water and cider until smooth.

3 Dip bread slices first in rice-milk mixture.

4 Then dip immediately into batter to coat both sides.

5 Melt margarine in a frying pan and fry bread slices on both sides until golden yellow. Keep slices warm while preparing syrup.

6 Cherry-red wine syrup: Brown 2 tbsp. of sugar in pan. Add margarine, cherries, red wine, and remaining sugar in this order and simmer on low heat until liquid thickens into a syrup.

Raspberry Crêpes

4 Servings

Crêpe batter:

7 oz. water (200 ml)

7 oz. cider or apple juice mixed with equal amount sparkling water (200 ml)

1¼ c. all-purpose flour (150 g)

1 tsp. sugar

⅛ tsp. salt

½ c. margarine (100 g)

Sauce:

9 oz. fresh or frozen raspberries (250 g)

2 oranges (organic)

1 lemon

3 tbsp. sugar or 2 tbsp. honey

½ c. white wine or apple juice (125 ml)

4 tbsp. margarine

Preparation time:

Approx. 40 min.

1 Crêpe batter: Whip flour, water, cider, salt and sugar in a bowl with wire whisk until smooth.

2 Crêpes: Melt 1 tsp. margarine in a pan and spoon in enough batter to thinly cover bottom of pan and cook on both sides until golden brown. Repeat process till batter is used up.

3 Sauce: Clean oranges thoroughly under hot water and thinly grate peel. Squeeze juice from oranges and lemon.

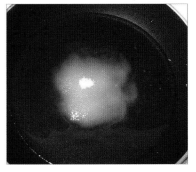

4 Melt margarine in pan, add sugar, stirring constantly until sugar is melted and lightly browned.

5 Add orange and lemon juice and grated peel. Pour in white wine and let simmer at low heat 10 min.

6 Fold crêpes into eighths. Place into orange sauce. Let stand in sauce for a few min. over low heat, turning several times. Arrange on plates, spread raspberries on top and serve warm.

Strawberries in Red Wine

4 Servings

1 ¹/₃ lb. small strawberries (600g)

¾ c. sugar (150 g)

17 oz. dry red wine (½ l)

Preparation time:

20 min.

Serving suggestion:

Serve with a coconut-vanilla sauce. (p.18)

1 Wash strawberries, drain and remove stems.

2 Place berries in a large bowl.

3 Sprinkle with sugar and pour wine on top.

4 Let stand at room temperature. Place berries in dessert bowls and serve.

Stuffed Dates

4 Servings

8 dried dates

3½ oz. walnuts (100 g)

¼ c. sugar (50 g)

2 tbsp. Grappa (grape brandy)

Preparation time:

Approx. 30 min.

1 Cut dates lengthwise along one side without cutting all the way through and remove pits. Finely chop walnuts in mixer.

2 Mix sugar, Grappa and walnuts well. Fill dates with this mixture, using a decorating pastry bag.

Banana-Nut Cake

One Cake

Batter:
4 1/8 c. flour (500 g)

1/2 c. sugar (100 g)

1/2 c. margarine (100 g)

3 1/2 oz. vegetable oil (100 ml)

Filling:
14 oz. nuts (400 g) and
3 medium bananas

3 1/2 oz. coconut milk or coconut
vanilla sauce, p. 18 (100 ml)

1/3 c. sugar (70 g)

Icing:
2 c. powdered sugar (250 g)

Juice of 1 lemon

Water, as needed

Slivered almonds to garnish

Preparation time:
1 1/2 hours
Preheat oven 340°F (170°C)

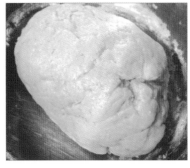

1 Blend flour, sugar, margarine, and vegetable oil and knead into a soft dough.

2 Set 1/3 dough aside. Press 2/3 dough into cake pan. Bake 10-15 min.

3 Coarsely chop nuts and mix with crushed bananas, 3 1/2 oz. (100 ml) coconut milk or sauce and sugar. Spread this mixture over baked dough. Roll out remaining dough and cover filling.

4 Puncture top dough many times with a fork. Place pastry in heated oven and bake 30 min. Blend ingredients for icing until smooth and spread over warm pastry. Top with slivered almonds.

Poppy Seed Pastry

One Cake

Batter: Recipe as above

Filling:
8 3/4 oz. poppy seeds (250 g)

4 1/4 c. rice milk (1 l)

7 tbsp. cornstarch or other thickener

2 oz. semolina or Farina or Cream of Wheat (60 g)

Preparation time:
Approx. 1 1/2 hours
Preheat oven 350°F (177° C)

1 Prepare pastry shell as above. Cook poppy seeds in 4 c. rice milk 15 min. until tender. Mix cornstarch with 1/2 c. cold rice milk. Add semolina and stir into cooking poppy-seed mixture.

2 Cool poppy seeds briefly. Spread poppy-seed mixture onto pastry shell. Bake 30 min.

Strawberry Torte

One Torte

Sponge cake:
$1\,2/3$ c. flour (200 g)
$2/3$ c. sugar (120 g)
1 ½ tsp. vanilla flavoring
3 tsp. baking powder
6 tbsp. sunflower oil
1 c. sparkling mineral water
(¼ l)
Grated rind of 1 lemon

Strawberry cream filling:
6 oz. vegan vanilla pudding or
vanilla sauce, p. 18 (180 g)
1/3 c. strawberry jam (100 g)
Juice of ½ lemon
6 tbsp. sugar
2 tsp. Amaretto

Garnish:
1 small bowl fresh strawberries
or other fruit
2 tbsp. slivered almonds

Preparation time:

Approx. 60 min.
Preheat oven 320°F
(160°-170°C)

1 Combine ingredients for sponge cake and whisk into a thick, but fluid batter. Grease a round cake pan well and sprinkle with bread crumbs or flour. Pour in cake batter.

2 Bake 20 to 25 min. Remove from pan and allow to cool.

3 Use mixer to blend ingredients for strawberry cream filling. Spread over top and sides of cooled sponge cake. Press slivered almonds onto the sides.

4 Wash and stem strawberries and arrange on top of cake. Decorate with the Torte-Cream (see recipe below).

Torte-Cream

4 Servings

1 ¼ c. margarine (250 g)
7 oz. coconut milk (200 ml)
½ c. sugar (100 g)
4 tbsp. cornstarch, or other
thickener
2 tsp. Amaretto or rum (10 ml)

Preparation time:

Approx. 30 min.

1 In a pan mix 5 oz. (150 ml) coconut milk with sugar. Bring to a boil. Dissolve cornstarch in 2 oz. (50 ml) coconut milk. Add to hot mixture and stir well. Season with amaretto or rum.

2 Cool hot mixture. Whip room temperature margarine until creamy. Add cooled coconut milk cream by the spoonfuls to make a fluffy cream.

Sweet Rolls

4 Servings

Dough:
4 1/8 c. flour (500 g)
1 packet dried yeast (20 g)
1/3 c. vegetable oil (80 g)
Pinch sugar
Pinch salt
7-8 oz. water (200-250 ml)
Grated rind of 1 lemon

Filling:
18 oz. grated apple (500 g)
7 oz. ground hazelnuts (200 g)
Pinch cinnamon
1 tsp. vanilla flavoring or
vanilla sugar

Glaze:
2 c. powdered sugar (250 g)
Juice of one lemon
Water as needed

Preparation time:

Approx. 40 min.
Preheat oven 150°F (70°C)

Variation:
Tastes delicious with a spicy filling for a party treat. Just spread the dough with a hearty tomato sauce containing lots of herbs.

1 Stir dry yeast and pinch sugar into ¼ c. lukewarm water (50 ml) and let stand a few min. Combine all ingredients for dough at room temperature and beat well until small bubbles appear and dough separates from edge of bowl.

2 Cover dough, place in a warm area and let rise ⅓ in volume. Meanwhile, mix ingredients for the filling well.

3 Roll dough ½ in. thick (1 cm). Cut ½ dough into squares, place small amount of apple filling on one half of square, fold over and press edges together. Make several cuts into sealed edge and bend uncut edge in the middle.

4 Roll out other ½ dough, spread with filling and roll together. Cut slices ½ in. thick (1 cm).

5 Place rolls on baking sheet, brush lightly with oil and let rise in preheated oven 10 min. Increase oven temperature to 340°F (170°C), bake 10-15 min. until golden brown.

6 For the glaze, blend powdered sugar, lemon juice until smooth. Add water if necessary. Glaze rolls while still hot from oven with this mixture.

Alphabetical Index

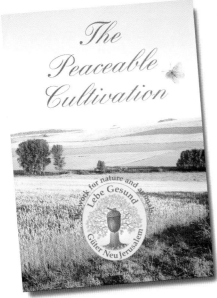

The Peaceable Cultivation

The Animal-Friendly Cookbook has made several references to the wholesomeness of the fruits of the fields grown under peaceable farming practices. To learn more about what this means, order a free copy of the brochure on Peaceable Cultivation.

Documentary Video Film:
There is an alternative to the violence of modern day farming in animal factory farming or the huge monoculture landscapes of agro-industry. Nature, in flora and fauna, suffer unbearably today at the hands of human beings. For this reason, a new approach is emerging that is based on high ethical moral values and which focuses on the unity of all life and on the divine order of creation.

Video Film, 30 min. $ 10.00 / Euro 8,00

THE WORD
THE UNIVERSAL SPIRIT
P.O. Box 3549
Woodbridge, CT 06525, USA
1-800-846-2691

Internet: www.Universal-Spirit.org

The Animal-Friendly Cookbook is published as commissioned by the

Gabriele-Stiftung

Gabriele-Foundation
The Saamlinic Work of Neighborly Love
for Nature and Animals
Your Kingdom come - Your Will Is Done
Pray and Work

The Sanctuary Land
A Home for Animals

It is important to the *Saamlinic Work of Neighborly Love for Nature and Animals* that animals are given a habitat in which they can lead a life that is worthy of the free creatures of God, in which they can run free and in peace, in a way that is species appropriate, without fear of being chased and tortured; that they live in a growing positive communication with human beings who go towards them with help and care, bringing them respect, esteem and friendship in feelings, thoughts and selfless deeds.

You can read more about this in the foreword of this Animal-Friendly Cookbook, or in the brochure that we would be happy to send you free of charge, upon request:

Gabriele-Foundation
Max-Braun-Str. 2
97828 Marktheidenfeld, Germany

www.Gabriele-Foundation.org

Books for You, for Nature and the Animals

This Is My Word
A and Ω
The Gospel of Jesus

The Christ-Revelation,
which meanwhile, true Christians
the world over have come to know

An inexhaustible work of revelation. What really happened 2000 years ago: The birth of Jesus, His life and works, His teaching, His sacrifice on Golgotha and His resurrection. Christ explains and deepens the true teaching of Jesus in a detailed way. He explains what spiritual processes lie behind the healings, the so-called miracles, the awakening of the dead and much more.

From the contents:
The origins of human beings and the Earth * Meaning and purpose of a life on Earth * The falsification of the teachings of Jesus over the past 2000 years * God never punishes or condemns, because He is the love * Jesus steadfastly stood up for the animals * The Sermon on the Mount * The sacrifice on Golgotha and the power of redemption in every soul * The path of self-recognition * The law of cause and effect * The life of the people in the Kingdom of Peace of Jesus Christ * and much more …

1078 pp., $ 19.99 / Euro 16,50
Order No. S 007en
ISBN: 978-1-890841-17-1

We will be happy to send you a free booklet of excerpts from this work of revelation so that you may get to know it.

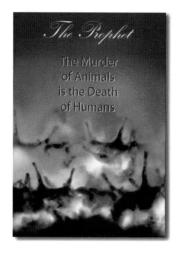

The Murder of Animals
Is the Death of Humans

Did we people really think there would be no effect from the centuries of ever more exploitation and pollution of our dwelling planet, the Earth, or from the disdain, torture and killing of God's creatures, the animals, in the most ignominious of ways? Then we have been deceiving ourselves, because now: the cup is full – it is enough! After all the horribleness committed by human beings to the animals and nature, the human being himself is on the line. The Prophet shows what this means with uncompromising clarity. Besides: Who is behind this destructive drive – and joins in?

60 pp., $ 2.00 / Euro 1,50

Animals Lament –
The Prophet Denounces!

Human beings torture, abuse and murder their fellow creatures, the animals. In this booklet, Gabriele lends a voice to the animals that also wants to speak to your heart. And, based on witnesses from old and new times, she points to the indescribable suffering of the animals and exposes the correlations and background to the millenia of disdain of animals that until now has been known to only a few, hardly having found any interest.

164 pp., color illustrations,
$ 3.00 / Euro 2,50
ISBN: 978-1-890841-43-0

People, don't eat us!
Please let us live!

A summarized exposé of all the reasons why eating meat is hazardous to our planet, hazardous to our health and, most especially, hazardous to the lives of our fellow creatures, the animals

16 pp., Order No. S 443en

The books on this page and a free catalog of all books and tapes from the Universal Spirit can be acquired by writing to:

THE WORD
THE UNIVERSAL SPIRIT
P.O. Box 3549
Woodbridge, CT 06525, USA
1-800-846-2691

Internet: www.Universal-Spirit.org